S0-DUU-944

Disability and
Christian Theology

AMERICAN ACADEMY OF RELIGION

Academy Series

SERIES EDITOR
Kimberly Rae Connor, University of San Francisco

A Publication Series of
The American Academy of Religion
and
Oxford University Press

Gregory of Nyssa and the Concept of Divine Persons
LUCIAN TURCESCU

Graham Greene's Catholic Imagination
MARK BOSCO, S.J.

Coming to the Edge of the Circle
A Wiccan Initiation Ritual
NIKKI BADO-FRALICK

The Ethics Of Animal Experimentation
A Critical Analysis and Constructive Christian Proposal
DONNA YARRI

Paul in Israel's Story
Self and Community at the Cross
JOHN L. MEECH

Crossing the Ethnic Divide
The Multiethnic Church on a Mission
KATHLEEN GARCES-FOLEY

God and the Victim
Traumatic Intrusions on Grace and Freedom
JENNIFER ERIN BESTE

The Creative Suffering of the Triune God
An Evolutionary Theology
GLORIA L. SCHAAB

A Theology of Criticism
Balthasar, Postmodernism, and the Catholic Imagination
MICHAEL P. MURPHY

Disability and Christian Theology
Embodied Limits and Constructive Possibilities
DEBORAH BETH CREAMER

AMERICAN ACADEMY OF RELIGION

Disability and Christian Theology

Embodied Limits and Constructive Possibilities

DEBORAH BETH CREAMER

OXFORD
UNIVERSITY PRESS

2009

OXFORD
UNIVERSITY PRESS

Oxford University Press, Inc., publishes works that further
Oxford University's objective of excellence
in research, scholarship, and education.

Oxford   New York
Auckland   Cape Town   Dar es Salaam   Hong Kong   Karachi
Kuala Lumpur   Madrid   Melbourne   Mexico City   Nairobi
New Delhi   Shanghai   Taipei   Toronto

With offices in
Argentina   Austria   Brazil   Chile   Czech Republic   France   Greece
Guatemala   Hungary   Italy   Japan   Poland   Portugal   Singapore
South Korea   Switzerland   Thailand   Turkey   Ukraine   Vietnam

Published by Oxford University Press, Inc.
198 Madison Avenue, New York, New York 10016

www.oup.com

Oxford is a registered trademark of Oxford University Press

Library of Congress Cataloging-in-Publication Data
Creamer, Deborah Beth.
Disability and Christian theology : embodied limits and constructive
possibilities / Deborah Beth Creamer.
    p. cm. — (Academy series)
Includes bibliographical references.
ISBN 978-0-19-536915-1
1. Body, Human—Religious aspects—Christianity.   2. Disabilities—
Religious aspects—Christianity.   I. Title.
BT741.3.C74 2009
261.8'324—dc22   2008017160

9 8 7 6 5 4 3 2 1

Printed in the United States of America
on acid-free paper

To Del Brown,
teacher and friend

Acknowledgments

This book proposes that human limits are unsurprising and that they are worthy of theological reflection. Writing a book is itself an experience in limits, where one faces unavoidable limits of time, sleep, and chocolate—as well as limits of knowledge and ability. It is only fitting that I preface this book by acknowledging and thanking those who helped me understand and adapt to my own limits and who gave generously of themselves. This project is much larger than anything I would have been able to accomplish alone.

Thank you to Sallie McFague and Joretta Marshall, who encouraged me to pursue my interest in disability and religion as part of my master's work, and to Delwin Brown, Sheila Davaney, Albert Hernández, and Frank Seeburger, who helped me develop these issues into the dissertation "The Withered Hand of God: Disability and Theological Reflection," upon which this book is based. Each made a substantial contribution not only to this project but also to my growth as a scholar. Special thanks to Sheila, an advisor in the best sense of the word, who helped map the way and who strengthened both the structure and content of my dissertation project.

This work would not exist in its current form without the support of Kimberly Rae Connor, editor of the AAR Academy Series, who guided me with care down the road from dissertation to book. I also wish to thank Oxford University Press, particularly Cynthia Read, Meechal Hoffman, and Jennifer Kowing, for their support of this project and their labor to bring it into being. I am grateful for the feedback of the anonymous reviewers (you know who you are!) as well as the non-anonymous folks—including Cathy Brown, Audrey Harris, Mary Olson, and Julie Todd—who willingly read and re-read my manuscript, helped me say more clearly what I meant, corrected the bibliographic citations, and developed the index.

The most extraordinary aspect of this process has been conversation. Whenever I have shared the ideas that follow—in classes, conferences, churches, and informal settings—people have freely offered their stories in response and have joined with me in reflecting on the diversity of our connections to disability and limits. Family, friends, acquaintances, and strangers, spread throughout the country and across a span of many years, are thus all contributors to this volume. Their conversational gifts immeasurably enrich this work. I am particularly grateful to my friends, colleagues, and students at the Iliff School of Theology who have encouraged and joined this conversation on many levels and who have been unfaltering supporters of my scholarly and professional journey. Lastly, and foundational to the scope of this work, have been my discussions with theorist and communication scholar Heidi Muller. These talks sparked a process of scholarship that continues today.

For all my conversation partners, I am deeply grateful.

Contents

Disability and Christian Theology

Introduction

Chances are very good that you know someone with a disability. Chances are also good that you have experienced—or will experience—some degree of disability yourself. In the United States, the Census Bureau estimates that approximately 18 percent of the population experience some degree of disability, and 12 percent experience a disability requiring assistance from a person or device.[1] Two in seven families are directly affected by disability.[2] Nationwide, 2.7 million people use a wheelchair, 1.8 million are reported as being unable to see, 1 million are reported as being unable to hear, and 14.3 million are reported to have limitations in cognitive functioning or a mental or emotional illness that interferes with their daily activities. Overall, 11 percent of children aged six to fourteen have a disability; 72 percent of people eighty and older have a disability.[3] The World Health Organization estimates that about 600 million people worldwide live with disabilities of various types.[4] Because disability is an "open minority" that any of us might join at any time, and which we are much more likely to join as we age, it has been suggested that it makes little sense to try to distinguish between able and disabled, but rather that any difference is simply between disabled and temporarily able-bodied. It is clear that disability is a common and ever-present experience that is worthy of theoretical and theological reflection.

To write about disability is to reconsider our understandings of human embodiment. In recent years, there has been an explosion of writing on the body—as Robyn Longhurst observes, the academy seems to be in the midst of a "body craze."[5] Important scholarly works on the body are appearing in such diverse fields as philosophy, culture and society, comparative literature, critical geography, history, bioethics, political theory, feminist studies, and countless others.[6] Not surprisingly, academic interest in the body appears throughout the disciplines of religious studies as well. Within the past ten years, for example, we have seen a profusion of works such as *Theology and the Body; Thealogy and Embodiment; Religious Reflections on the Human Body; Begin with the Body; Religion and the Body; Body and Soul;* and *The Good News of the Body.*[7] While the expanding interest in the human body—including its many variations (sexuality, gender, race, and so on) and its complex material/historical nature—is an exciting academic trend, the picture of what is meant by "body" is still only beginning to come into focus.

Unfortunately, even in the midst of this body craze, most scholars who explore human embodied existence seem to assume a "healthy" body to be the norm.[8] This has two substantial implications. First, even as we begin to attend seriously to the embodied insights of particularities such as race, gender, ethnicity, sexuality, and other characteristics, we leave an important aspect of embodied existence unexamined if we overlook reflection on the experience of disability. Second, just as scholars have noted that it is extremely problematic to examine only men within our exploration of race, or only whites within our exploration of gender, it is similarly problematic to attend only to the nondisabled within any of these other embodiment discourses. In other words, we are not only lacking a scholarship of ability/disability; we are also erroneous in our scholarship of other particularities when we fail to attend to disability and nondisability. We must pay serious attention to the fluidity and variety of instantiations of human ability if we are to engage in an authentic project of critical reflection on the substance and significance of bodies.

In the chapters that follow, we will not only explore the contributions made by reflection on disability but also witness that these are theologically meaningful and valuable perspectives with relevance beyond the realm of "people with disabilities." As with insights that have come from attentive engagement with other marginalized perspectives, theological reflection on disability has the potential to challenge theological injustices, as well as to offer new theological contributions.

The Ad/Vantage of Disability

It has become an expectation in written works on disability to begin with an identification of where the author falls on the disability continuum, in particular to include a "coming out" as to whether she claims the label "disabled" for herself. Just as members of the Deaf community have traditionally introduced themselves to strangers with both their names and the identity of the school they attended, so participants in disability studies are expected to begin their scholarly work by pairing their name with an identification of their disability status. In both cases, this is understood as intimately related to the individual's authority and credibility. According to many, one must be disabled to speak legitimately about disability. At the annual meeting of the American Academy of Religion in 2003, for example, a number of audience members in a session of the Religion and Disability Studies group (including some particularly distinguished scholars) questioned the legitimacy of those who presented papers or asked questions as "outsiders" (those without "sufficient" personal experience with disability) or as "affiliates" (those who are the parent, partner, or child of a person with a disability).[9] As has been seen in other movements, there is an essentialist strain, a tendency to enact identity politics. A recurring question is: Can someone without disabilities ever understand what it is to be disabled? This leads to another question: How disabled must one be to count as having authority on this issue? Intertwined with these epistemological questions is an intense concern that the discourse of disability studies should be controlled by people with disabilities—a sometimes legitimate fear of colonialism and misappropriation by others.[10]

Is this an epistemological privilege of disability? Are there knowledges that people with disabilities possess but which are lacking in those who are nondisabled? Or do we all know these things, even though we sometimes forget? This book suggests that the appropriate answer is yes to both of these questions. Yes, reflection on experiences of disability offers a vantage or, more accurately, multiple vantages that are often lacking and that have the potential to enhance both theory and practice. Yes, also, we must not forget that all of us—disabled and nondisabled—are embodied creatures. While it is inaccurate and potentially harmful (as will be discussed in chapter 1) to say naively that "we are all disabled," it is also important to remember that most of us have had some sort of experience with pain and limitation and impairment, and that most of us will experience disability more fully as we age. This double yes to particularity and universality serves to complicate the question of "does the author have—or need to have—a disability?"

To add another layer of complexity to this insider/outsider debate, as Tanya Titchkosky notes, "Any experience of disability includes others' understandings of it."[11] Disability identity, as both a label and a form of self-understanding, depends a great deal on the interpretations of others. One is disabled insofar as he or she appears disabled. I am disabled, perhaps, when I use my cane. In some ways, such classification follows from the history of disability itself—to be disabled is to be labeled so, typically by a medical practitioner or social service/governmental agency. In this way, disability identity is intricately related to medical, economic, and political issues. Similar relationships can be seen within other identities. For example, as feminist theory has shown, what it is to be a woman has been inextricably linked to the ways and degree to which one is seen and treated as a woman. To be a person with a disability has much to do with the extent and degree to which one is understood or treated as having a disability. Disability identity also depends on societal understandings of normal, reminiscent of Foucault's studies of madness where the concept of sanity is seen to have no meaning without the realization of its opposite, insanity.[12]

Yet even these external categorizations are not as simple as they might seem. For example, neither the category disabled nor the category nondisabled fits particularly well for me.[13] I pass, and pass rather well, in both but fit comfortably in neither. I match neither the understandings and expectations of "normal" nor the common assumptions of "disabled" that come from external medical or societal sources, and neither category seems to capture or make sense of my own internal and embodied experiences. Interestingly, though, when I refuse to claim explicitly either of these two categories for myself, I often find them to be chosen for me. To illustrate, as a way of introducing a chapter I wrote for a book on disability and theological education, the editor stated that my article drew from my "experience as a minister, theologian and person with a disability."[14] This claim was not based on anything I had said about myself, but rather on the assumption that someone who writes on this topic must have a personal experience with disability. In other locations, such as the academic institution where I work, I am assumed to be a nondisabled person with only a theoretical interest in these issues because I do not show visible signs of disability with consistency. Yet neither of these assumptions matches my own experiences.

This ambiguity in perception is part of what has brought me to the limits model that I propose and explore in this book.[15] The term "disability," as it is commonly used, is an absolute category without levels or thresholds. One is either disabled or not. From this perspective, "one cannot be a little disabled any more than one can be a little pregnant."[16] The two prevalent models in disability studies (medical and minority, which will be explained in detail in chapter 1) offer no alternative to this either/or perspective. Yet reflection on the lived experiences of people who identify as disabled, as well as those who do not, shows the reality of disability to be significantly more complex and fluid than the category suggests. Lennard Davis is one of the few within disability studies to speak of the need for an alternative to conventional static notions of disability. For Davis, "what we are discussing is the instability of the category of disability as a subset of the instability of identity in a postmodern era."[17] As part of the challenge that destabilizes unifying theories and problematizes unity and wholeness, disability may be a category that is no longer relevant in a postmodern world. This move to highlight the constructed and somewhat arbitrary nature of the category, however, makes many disability scholars and most disability rights activists quite nervous. Davis relates hearing from a prominent disability scholar that "We're not ready to dissolve disability identity. We're just beginning to form it."[18] It does make sense that there is a strategy behind identity politics, especially during the early stages of an academic or political movement. It is only in recent years that people with disabilities have been able to seize the term "disability" in an attempt to control its usage. For the purposes of self-identification, academic and political access, and other liberative agendas, an exclusive understanding of disability identity may have strategic value. But even in this quest for justice, we must not let reflection on the complexity of human embodiment fall by the wayside.

Beyond making more accurate sense of lived experiences of people with and without disabilities, this challenge to the category of able/disabled may offer us a way to rethink identity dilemmas in other situations as well. There are times when we might look back nostalgically to the age when identity seemed relatively simple, when it was possible to say that one *was* black or white, male or female—but issues of identity by race, gender, or sexual orientation, particularly in the United States, have become more complicated than perhaps they used to be. This complexity can also be seen within the issue of disability. As Davis notes:

> Disability is not a minor issue that relates to a relatively small number of unfortunate people; it is part of a historically constructed discourse, an ideology of thinking about the body under certain historical circumstances. Disability is not an object—a woman with a cane—but a social process that intimately involves everyone who has a body and lives in the world of the senses. Just as the conceptualization of race, class, and gender shapes the lives of those who are not black, poor, or female, so the concept of disability regulates the bodies of those who are "normal." In fact, the very concept of normalcy by which most people (by definition) shape their existence is in fact tied inexorably to the concept of disability, or rather, the concept of disability is a function of a concept of normalcy. Normalcy and disability are part of the same system.[19]

As with other categories, the concept of disability is integrally related to structures of power and is dependent on sociopolitical categories constructed by an ableist culture. Thus the object of disability studies is most accurately not the person using the wheelchair but rather the sets of social, historical, economic, and cultural processes that regulate and control the way we think about and through the body. This does not mean that we should do away with handicapped parking spots or repeal the provisions of the Americans with Disabilities Act. Even in a postmodern world, curb cuts and closed-captioning are still important. Deconstructing the category "disability" does not erase embodied experience such as pain or physical limitation. Yet we must recognize that even these elements of disability are not solely "individual" experiences but rather are rich with communal and societal input and implication.

Awareness of issues of identity hermeneutics calls for a reexamination of the category "disability," especially insofar as this category has profound implications for self-identity, communal identity, and theological identity. It is not solely an individual issue. Thus, when confronted with the question of self-identity and authority, Davis responds in this way: "My aim is to confound the question and by extension the category that the question begs. And my answer is not, and should not be, clear."[20] In stating my location for this work, I must offer a similar reply. I am aware that I must check an EEOC box on employment forms that allow me only a "yes" or "no" as to my disability status, with no room for an asterisk referencing my reflection on disability and human limits. I know that the editor's matter-of-fact introduction to my chapter will precede my job interviews, as will reference letters from faculty who have never broached the topic of why I use a cane on some days and not on others. Approaching the subject of disability, I know that there are some relevant experiences I have had and many, many others that I have not.[21] Also, like any other writer, I know that what follows is the result of many aspects of my identity, both personal and academic. As a result, I offer my reflections here as a preliminary response to a complex constellation of issues, and simultaneously offer an invitation to the reader to join with me as a partner in conversation to which you bring your own experiences and commitments. This, too, embodies the claim that disability is not just an individual experience—it is, at least in part, socially and theologically constructed, and thus any reflection on disability should similarly be understood as necessarily more than any single individual's perspective.

There is, I argue, an ad/vantage that comes from the experience of disability. From my own physical limitations and chronic pain, I know things about the world that others do not seem to know; I have had experiences and have gained perspectives that allow me to challenge the invisibility and obscuration of embodied difference. Yet, given that disability is manifest in so many forms, and given that all people experience embodiment and limits, this vantage is not, nor should it be, the only perspective to shape theological reflection on diverse embodiment. Personal experience of disability allows us to perceive and express perspectives that are often overlooked or forgotten. But, as we have learned from feminist and other liberation processes, these personal experiences need communal conversation and reflection to become anything more than untranslatable individual claims to truth and knowledge.

Linguistic and Experiential Dangers

An important caveat to highlight at the beginning of this sort of project is that neither talking about disability nor reflecting on experiences of disability is as simple—or as neutral—as it might initially seem. As has been alluded to earlier, most people are fairly comfortable in their commonsense understanding of what is meant by disability. This meaning-making is tied to societal understandings of normalcy. When we talk about disability or label someone disabled, we know what we mean. But as we enter this project, it is important to remember that the use of the word "disability" is deceptive, especially insofar as it acts to condense what is in fact a complex constellation of definitions and experiences, and inasmuch as any appeal to experience (including "the experience of disability") is problematic. As we will see, talking about disability is no easy thing.

One danger comes from the deceptive simplicity of the term "disabled" itself. Chapter 1 demonstrates how this term has been used to characterize a wide variety of experiences (including sensory, mobility, cognitive, and emotional differences), and chapter 2 shows that even this cluster has changed dramatically over time. Disability is, in this sense, a sort of illusion, and one that can be dangerous if used to make visible some instantiations of "difference" and negate others. We see this most clearly by examining discussions of naming in feminist theology, and particularly in the early use of the label "woman."[22] As bell hooks and others have noted, "woman" has too often been used to mean only a certain kind of woman: "Much feminist theory emerges from privileged women who live at the center, whose perspectives on reality rarely include knowledge and awareness of the lives of women and men who live in the margin."[23] This lack of wholeness has had specific implications; for example, hooks notes that "women in lower class and poor groups, particularly those who are nonwhite, would not have defined women's liberation as women gaining social equality with men."[24] Feminist theology must continually struggle with the meaning and the usefulness of the term "woman." Similarly, disability studies must be attentive that use of the word "disabled" necessarily includes a wide number of "disability experiences" as well as a constellation of other identities (including gender, race, class, and so on).

Beyond the diversity of disability itself, the appeal to the "experience of disability" holds within it many of the dangers encountered with other appeals to particular experiences. Sharon Welch suggests that, while appeals to experience have been useful, for example, in giving voice (academic and otherwise) to women of color, we must remember that experience cannot be drawn upon as an innocent or "truthful" source of knowledge. Welch argues that "feminists who appeal to women's experience are making a hermeneutical—not a metaphysical—claim."[25] She asks that we identify the appeal to experience as an invitation, as the beginning of a conversation, rather than any sort of solid conclusion. For Welch, this is key to what she calls an ethic of criticism, where power arises not in any imagined truth but rather "from processes of listening, inventing, and responding to very particular challenges, to very particular lives and opportunities."[26]

Given this discussion, two dangers of the appeal to the experience of disability immediately present themselves as we engage this work. First, we must be attentive that there is no single "experience of disability"; similarly, there is no single "experience of wheelchair use" or "experience of college students paralyzed in skiing accidents." Experience is a diverse and multivocal category, and it is an unfortunate consequence of written academic work that such multivocality is often lost. Given the choice between particularity ("theology and the experience of skiing injuries") and broad categories ("theology and disability"), I have focused on the latter, with the hope that individual differences not be lost or whitewashed,[27] but rather used as particular lenses through which to view the overall project. A second danger emerges when we recognize, through Welch's nudging, that there is no innocent knowledge. People with disabilities are just as socially conditioned as anyone else, which thus suggests an argument against an intrinsic epistemological privilege. I agree with bell hooks that there is, in many cases, a "special vantage point our marginality gives us," which can be useful as we seek to "envision and create a counter-hegemony."[28] Many people with disabilities have had the opportunity to see life from the underside and have perspectives that have not yet been acknowledged in the greater academic or social structures. There is a contribution to be made, but we must not forget that it is not an uncomplicated one. As Sheila Briggs reminds us, the identities of class, gender, and race (and, I would add, disability) are all mediated by social practices.[29]

This suspicion of an intrinsic epistemological privilege combined with the fluidity of disability leads me to the claim that any theology of disability must include the voices and perspectives both of those who identify as disabled and of those who do not. This is, perhaps, similar to the claim that there can be a place for men in the feminist movement. Sandra Bartky notes three possible rationales for making such a claim: men have been harmed by antifeminist thought; justice demands that no one (including men) be excluded; and practical political concerns call for men's participation. As she writes, "Given the antiquity, power, depth, and breadth of patriarchy, I doubt that women alone can overthrow it. We need 'gender traitors,' and lots of them, to effect a thoroughgoing reform of our institutions."[30] I have described this book as a reflection on disability and theology, but my earlier discussion demands that the participants not be limited to those who take or have been given the name "disabled" as a descriptor of their own identity or experiences. This project is not simply of the disabled or for the disabled. Reflection on the intersection of disability and theology has implications for us all (we have all been harmed by conceptions of disability), our focus on inclusion demands that we exclude no one, and we clearly need "ability traitors" as well as disability advocates to help counter ingrained notions of normality.

Goals for the Project

In the pages that follow, we will explore the theological contributions that come from engagement with disability and human limits, providing an analysis of the current state of such engagement as well as proposals for the future of such work. After exploring possible meanings of "disability" and then reviewing relationships between disability and the Christian tradition, we will explore these constructive possibilities in three concrete ways: first, by exploring how existing theological models might be expanded to include disability; second, by considering liberation theologies of disability; and third, by imagining new possibilities for a theology that grows uniquely out of reflection on disability. All three approaches complicate our commonsense notions of normal and disabled and present a challenge for us and others working on issues of embodiment and theology to reflect upon and to represent the experiences and perspectives of actual bodies in all their lived and constructed diversity.

Critical reflection on the diversity of human embodiment has the potential to keep us grounded—embodied as it were—in an understanding of what human limits enable and what they make difficult. Such grounding offers a significant contribution to the field of disability studies, which otherwise lacks a perspective from which to incorporate the full diversity of individual situations and reactions to experiences of limits. A similar contribution is offered to the field of theology, especially insofar as it enables us to reflect on theological and anthropological implications of the undeniable diversity of human embodiment and the pervasiveness of human limits. This perspective is essential for theology, both as we contribute our reflections to issues of justice and also as we seek new images and possibilities for theological construction that are compatible with diverse experiences of human embodiment.

I

Understanding Disability

Before we consider the various ways in which disability might intersect with theological reflection, we must first try to make sense of disability itself. Our first significant challenge comes from a rather benign resistance to this task: to most people, defining disability seems unnecessary. As Rosemarie Garland Thomson notes, disability and able-bodiedness seem to be "self-evident physical conditions."[1] It seems strange to even ask what disability is. We can describe it, draw pictures of it, point out examples of it. We think that we know (or can imagine) what it means to "be disabled." It is a category that makes sense to us. Perhaps most tellingly, we often think that we know (usually just by looking) if someone is disabled, and we think that we know if someone is not. Disability seems to be a self-evident category. But is it?

What Is Disability?

Definitions and Statistics

In the current scholarship of disability studies, distinctions are often drawn between terms such as "impairment," "disability," and "handicap." "Impairment" usually signifies an abnormality or loss of physiological form or function. For example, a damaged optical nerve is classified as an impairment. "Disability" describes the consequences of the impairment, which may be an inability to perform some task or activity. In this example, the disability might be an inability to see. "Handicap," literally meaning "to hinder" or "to place at a disadvantage," denotes the disadvantage that results from an impairment or disability. A person is considered handicapped, for example, when the damaged optical nerve or the inability to see makes one unable to distinguish floor numbers on elevator buttons, thus hindering navigation without additional assistance. While we may most often think of these three terms as inextricably linked (i.e., that a person with a significant impairment is both disabled and handicapped), it is important to note that an impairment does not necessarily result in a disability, and a disability need not be a handicap. Our hypothetical friend with the damaged optical nerve (an impairment) would not be handicapped if the elevator buttons were marked in Braille and would not be disabled (the impairment would have no consequences) in the dark.

In the United States today, our use of the term "disability" often draws on the language of the Americans with Disabilities Act of 1990, which defines disability as "a physical or mental impairment that substantially limits one or more of the major life activities" of an individual.[2] According to the U.S. Census Bureau, "a person is considered to have a disability if he or she has difficulty performing certain functions, or has difficulty performing activities of daily living, or has difficulty with certain social roles."[3] While these definitions usually exclude temporary illnesses, they encompass a wide variety of physical, cognitive, and psychological impairments. Using such definitions, it is currently estimated that 51.2 million Americans have some level of physical or mental disability (18 percent of the population), and 3.2 million have a severe disability (12 percent of the population).[4]

Even though disability is found in all age-groups, issues of disability should be of particular concern as the population ages due to worldwide changes in fertility and mortality (fewer children are born, and more people reach old age) and as the baby boom generation approaches retirement.[5] For example, the World Health Organization projects that by the year 2020, the proportion of population aged sixty and over will reach 23 percent in North America, and the total number of elderly people worldwide will reach more than 1 billion. In addition to other social and economic implications, population aging means that "more and more people will be entering the age when the risk of developing certain chronic and debilitating diseases is significantly higher."[6] Not only, then, do we need to attend to disability today, but we must also consider the growing impact it will have in years to come.

Disability beyond the Statistics

While they may give us a starting point in terms of understanding the frequency of disability, statistics fail to represent the diversity found within the category "disabled." If we pay attention, it does not take us long to see that disability takes many forms and affects human lives in a wide variety of ways, to the point that using the single term "disability" to lump together people who experience mobility impairment, sensory loss, disfigurement, chronic pain, long-term illness, developmental difference, dyslexia, schizophrenia, depression, and more, is to create a deceptively simple category. Moreover, even within any single particular condition, there is often a great deal of variety. For example, disability (impairment) may be temporary or permanent. It may affect all aspects of an individual's life or may be a fairly minor inconvenience. Impairment may result from accident, illness, or genetics, or the cause may be unknown. Some people have their conditions from birth; others acquire them in youth, adulthood, or old age. Certain impairments are relatively stable, others become progressively worse, and some improve with time or medical intervention. People with disabilities may use very different technologies to adapt to their situations or may "pass" without any apparent aid. In addition, it is important to recognize that people with disabilities are not all treated the same by the nondisabled, especially since some disabilities are more socially acceptable than others, and individuals may have very dissimilar attitudes toward their own conditions. In these and many other ways, the "experience of disability" is diverse indeed!

Beyond this, it is important to remember that people with disabilities have other characteristics as well. Disability crosses all lines of race, gender, sexual orientation, class, age, and so on. These and other life experiences affect each person's experience of disability. Sometimes the relationship between disability and other identities is direct, as when poverty or malnutrition leads to a disabling condition or prevents a person from receiving medical treatment or adaptive technologies. Conversely, disability can lead to poverty if a person either is physically unable to work or is denied the right to work by barriers of access or attitude. Other times the relationship between identities is less immediate but still important. A young person and an older person might respond to a similar disability in very different ways. A businessperson may have an easier time adapting to mobility impairment than a professional athlete. Issues of race, class, gender, and sexual orientation affect the sorts of barriers and obstacles a person with a disability will face, and people who experience oppression or exclusion as members of one or more of these minority groups may find themselves doubly (or triply) oppressed as a result of their disability.

One particular area of concern in contemporary scholarship has been the interaction between sexism and disability.[7] Until recently, research has paid little attention to women with disabilities; most studies on disability have focused on men's issues and have used male subjects, with results (at least, until recently) assumed to be normative for both men and women. The omission of women's health issues from medical research has recently come to the attention of the general public (e.g., we are only beginning to learn about causes and characteristics of heart disease in women); these gaps in research are particularly significant for women with disabilities. In addition to medical issues, women's narrative experiences of disability have also received less attention in scholarship than those of men. Some propose that this is because disability is culturally interpreted as more traumatic and life changing for men than for women, especially insofar as disability in men, at least within Western culture, is seen as a lack of ability (a tangible loss, with specific economic implications), whereas disability in women instead is seen as a loss or lack of beauty (and, often, a loss of potential as a wife or mother). Others propose that disability in men has been seen as more significant insofar as disability often is equated with dependency, and traditional stereotypes seem to suggest that it is more acceptable for a woman to be or appear dependent than it is for a man. It is clearly erroneous, however, to assume that disability is less traumatic for women than for men. For example, compared with both nondisabled women and men with disabilities, women with disabilities typically have a lower level of educational achievement, a higher rate of unemployment, and, for those who are employed, a significantly lower annual income. Noting the limited role choices and limited role models available to disabled women, Michelle Fine and Adrienne Asch go so far as to conclude that "disability is a more severely handicapping condition for women than for men."[8]

The needs and issues of women with disabilities have largely been ignored by the disabled rights movement; men have held the power in these organizations and have, intentionally or not, determined which issues are to be given priority. As Mary Jo Deegan and Nancy Brooks note, "Like many other social change movements, the disability movement has often directed its energies toward primarily male experiences."[9] Concerns of women with disabilities— including discrimination as a result of gender and disability, violence against women with disabilities, and sexism within their organizations—have been disregarded. While this is beginning to change as women take leadership roles and demand that our concerns be addressed, change is slow.

Unfortunately, the feminist movement has been no better than the disability rights movement at attending to or engaging with disabled women. Events and meetings are often not physically accessible, and women with disabilities who are present are frequently encouraged to work on "their own issues" with "their own kind."[10] As Pat Israel recounts: "Years ago when I attended a national women's conference I had to use a dirty, foul-smelling freight elevator to get to the workshops. There was garbage on the floor and walls. I felt degraded and dirty every time I had to use it. I wonder what would have happened if the black women had been told to use the freight elevator because they were black."[11] While organizations are now more aware of and sensitive to issues of access, necessary adaptations are still often made only after a member requests such services (e.g., meetings are rarely interpreted into sign language as a matter of course, and convention sites still frequently include barriers to mobility). Going beyond issues of access, areas of tension arise between disabled and nondisabled feminists over issues such as abortion, caregiving, and technology. For example, many women with disabilities identify themselves as feminists but reject a pro-choice position on abortion, arguing that abortion is too often used as a form of eugenics against disability; this position is difficult for many nondisabled feminists to understand or accept.[12] Thus, even when issues of basic accessibility are addressed, other diversities of identity and political commitments are frequently overlooked.

This nascent literature on women and disabilities also reminds us of the lack of attention to disability in relation to other identity concerns. For example, little has been written to date on disability and race or on disability and sexual orientation. We must be mindful that disability is not an exclusive category but rather one that intersects all other identity and interest groups. Similarly, we must take care that we not assume one individual or group experience of disability to be typical or representative of all people with disabilities. People with disabilities are as different as people without disabilities. Alan Gartner and Tom Joe perceptively write:

> It is mistaking the diversity of persons with disabilities to expect or desire that they all will have the same views or values. Some are Yankees fans, others favor the Mets; some are men, others women; some are black, others white; many are poor but some affluent; some politically liberal, others conservative; some see gains won primarily from individual efforts, others from group action. On many, indeed most, issues, it will be these (and other) factors, not the fact of the person's disability, which will have the most salience.[13]

People with disabilities are individuals—individuals with different attitudes toward their disabilities, individuals with different sociological influences and characteristics, individuals with different political positions, individuals with different tastes and interests. It is important that we remember that there is no one perspective that can be called "the disabled person's perspective."

It is a challenge to be mindful of this diversity: it is too easy to assume one perspective—usually our own—to be normative and to create interpretations and doctrine based on experiences that do not represent the full diversity of the people to whom, or for whom, we speak. However, as feminist and liberation theologians so clearly demonstrate, diversity includes a richness that can be an asset, not a liability, to our understandings of ourselves and of God.[14] The same is true for the diversity of disability. Each perspective is different, but each offers us a piece of the puzzle. Susan Brooks Thistlethwaite and Mary Potter Engel remark that "people look alike only when you cannot be bothered to look at them closely."[15] Beyond the most obvious signs of accommodation (wheelchair, hearing aid), many people choose not to look closely at those with disabilities. By ignoring these differences, we not only miss truly encountering one another but also miss important truths about ourselves and the world.

Finally, in addition to seeing disability as a category that holds immense diversity within it, we must note that the category itself is an unstable one, with no neat differentiation between "us" and "them." The most obvious example of this is seen when we consider that disability will likely impact each of us during the course of our lives. Disability has been called an "open minority" because it is a group that most of us will "join" at some point in our lives.[16] Even if one does not live long enough to experience a significant disability, most of us will have some sort of firsthand experience with impairment, whether it be a sprained ankle, the need for eyeglasses, or the "normal" limitations that come as we age. As Elizabeth Stuart notes, "The contrast is not between the able and disabled but between the temporarily able and the disabled."[17] However, while the recognition of this fluidity can be valuable in expanding our perspectives and breaking down some of the dichotomy between able and disabled, it is also important that we do not appeal to this fluidity to minimize the legitimate justice concerns of people with disabilities. Using a wheelchair for a week can teach an able-bodied person a lot about what it is like to be disabled, but it cannot teach her what it is to be a lifelong wheelchair user; it would be inappropriate to say a person could understand everything about the experience of disability from an isolated experience of impairment. At the same time, the wheelchair user-for-a-week might have a better understanding of mobility impairment than a person who has been deaf from birth and has always been identified as disabled. As we recognize these sorts of interweaving connections and differences, we can begin to realize a significant truth: we may in some important ways be more alike than different, even though we are different in significant ways.

Disability and Activism

While it is outside the scope of this work to present a complete history of disability and disability studies, a brief overview of this topic may be helpful.[18] Throughout much of history, people with disabilities have been oppressed and repressed as individuals and as a social group. People with disabilities have been isolated, incarcerated, institutionalized, and controlled. Without entering into any sort of "oppression derby" over which minority group has been the most oppressed in history, it is important to note that people with disabilities, especially those who experience double or triple oppression based on other categories of gender, race, class, and so on, have experienced some of the worst that history has had to offer. People with disabilities have been defined as many things: deserving victims of divine punishment, objects of scorn, sideshow freaks, medical case studies, recipients of charity, and poster children. In movies and in literature (and perhaps most clearly in children's stories), disability has been used as a metaphor both for evil and for childlike innocence, and disabled people have frequently been portrayed as malevolent, comical, or victims of a fate worse than death.[19] As has been the case for other minority groups, rarely have people with disabilities been viewed first as people.

Examples of prejudice and discrimination are too numerous to mention, but a few instances will set the scene. In the nineteenth and early twentieth centuries, many states passed laws forbidding people with particular disabilities to marry, and some disabled people were forcibly sterilized. In 1927, the U.S. Supreme Court heard arguments on the forced sterilization of people with disabilities who were wards of the state.[20] In an eight-to-one decision, the Court allowed the sterilization to proceed, with Chief Justice Oliver Wendell Holmes writing that "it is better for all the world, if instead of waiting to execute degenerate offspring for crime, or to let them starve for their imbecility, society can prevent those who are manifestly unfit from continuing their kind."[21] In addition to such attempts at eugenics, people with disabilities have been routinely incarcerated, sometimes for life, in institutions and nursing homes, solely because of their disabilities.[22] A 1911 Chicago city ordinance (known as the "Chicago Ugly Law") went so far as to make it a crime for anyone who was "in any way deformed so as to be an unsightly or disgusting object" to appear in public.[23]

People with disabilities in the United States have been organizing for more than a century to fight such injustices. As early as the 1850s, local organizations were established to advocate for the interests of deaf people, leading to the formation of the National Association of the Deaf in 1880. During the Great Depression, the League of the Physically Handicapped staged sit-ins at federal offices to protest antidisability discrimination by government programs. The National Federation of the Blind and the American Federation of the Physically Handicapped were organized in the early 1940s, and disabled soldiers returning home after World War II founded the Paralyzed Veterans of America. Around the same time, parents of disabled children began to form self-help groups that later grew into national advocacy organizations. Polio and spinal cord injury survivors asserted their right to study, work, and live in communities, and people with psychiatric disabilities protested custodial institutions. Inspired by the African American civil rights movement and the women's movement, various disability communities began to coalesce in the 1960s, giving rise to the modern disability rights movement. Finally, in the early 1970s, a series of legal cases, first and foremost *PARC v. Commonwealth of Pennsylvania,* crystallized disability as a civil rights issue.[24] In the decades since, disability rights advocates have scored numerous significant legal and legislative victories, culminating in passage of the Americans with Disabilities Act of 1990.

Alongside these political movements has been the growth of a disability culture that challenges traditional notions and assumptions about disability. Disabled artists, writers, performers, and activists celebrate disability as a facet of human diversity. It is now easy to find television and movies that focus on issues of disability and/or include characters with disabilities.[25] People with disabilities are also gaining unprecedented access to public life and serving in significant roles in business, government, and education. However, as millions of disabled Americans remain locked in poverty and as barriers of attitude and architecture keep people with disabilities from full participation in society, the disability movement still centers on legal challenges, protests, and activism of all sorts.

Disability and the Academy

A significant addition to the disability movement as a whole has been the development of the academic discipline of disability studies, giving the opportunity for theoretical reflection, critique, and construction that not only contributes to the academy but may also act to sustain the movement as it looks beyond legal issues of access and inclusion. The field grew out of the work of disabled scholars and activists in the 1980s and 1990s who found that disability, as a socially constructed phenomenon, was not being critically addressed within traditional academic disciplines. Disability studies emphasizes the articulation and theorization of the political, social, and ideological ways in which disability is understood, treated, and experienced. Current work focuses on a critique of the "essential" disabled person and an exploration of the various ways in which people are socially constructed by disabling environments. While access remains a primary issue of concern, many of these more recent scholarly productions are concerned with identity construction beyond actual experiences of limitation. For example, Rosemarie Garland Thomson, one of the key figures in disability studies, describes a recent project as an attempt to "go beyond assailing stereotypes to interrogate the conventions of representation and unravel the complexities of identity production within social narratives of bodily difference."[26] Others emphasize "the implications of disability representations from the perspective of the disability rights movement,"[27] or how "the disabled use, elude, resist, or rewrite the culturally authorized scripts of disability identity."[28] This cross-disciplinary enterprise of theorizing experiences and constructions of disability draws from a wide variety of fields, including sociology, anthropology, political science, literature and film studies, philosophy, psychology, architecture and design, and the arts.

Like any other discipline, disability studies requires a base of knowledge and a familiarity with discursive terms and methodologies. While defining itself as a scholarly academic pursuit, it also sees itself as a logical progression from the disability rights movement and as such is careful not to lose its grounding in praxis. Lennard Davis writes, "It is not as if disability studies has simply appeared out of someone's head at this historical moment. It would be more appropriate to say that disability studies has been in the making for years, but, like people with disabilities, has only recently recognized itself as a political, discursive entity."[29] As has been the case with the civil rights movement or the feminist movement, there is understood to be a reciprocal connection between political praxis by people with disabilities and the formation of a discursive category of disability studies.

However, like race and gender studies, disability studies is not a monolithic undertaking but rather is the site of internal struggle and debate over its desired identity, methodology, and commitments. One particularly heated topic at present regards what qualifies one as an expert. For example, it is frequently argued that some degree of personal involvement with the experience of disability is necessary. People without disabilities (sometimes playfully or pejoratively referred to as TABs—temporarily able-bodied) are often regarded with suspicion as to their motivation or ability to understand the full scope of the field. For example, one author writes that "the apparent ease of intuitive knowledge is really another aspect of discrimination against people with disabilities."[30] While rarely articulated as such, the legitimacy of an epistemic privilege of people with disabilities is becoming a central concern in the field of disability studies.

At the same time an argument is made by some that disability studies ought to be limited to those with personal experiences of disability, the work of many other scholars who have investigated various aspects of the body and related issues is also being appropriated by the field of disability studies. Examples of these sources include Sander Gilman's work on disease, David Rothman on asylums, Erving Goffman on stigma, Leslie Fiedler on freaks, Susan Sontag on the metaphors of illness, Mikhail Bakhtin on the grotesque, Michel Foucault on disease and sexuality, Jacques Derrida on blindness, Judith Butler on gender and sexuality, and Susan Bordo on anorexia.[31] As the field of disability studies evolves, it works backward to incorporate historical writings on disease, the body, freakishness, and so on, while it simultaneously looks forward to a new generation of writers and scholars interested in feminist, Marxist, postmodern, and cultural studies models for understandings of the relation between the body and power.

As those who work with issues of disability in the academy and on the picket lines continue to define and defend their goals and commitments, they, along with those who watch them, still return again and again to our first question: What is disability? We turn now to two very different answers to that question, as seen in the medical and minority models. We will discover that these perspectives are only partially adequate, which will lead us to the limits model as an alternate way to attend to the experience of disability.

Models of Disability

Medical or Functional-Limitation Model

As suggested previously, disability may be best seen less as a precise category (where one either is or is not disabled) and more as a broad descriptive term for a cluster of somewhat related experiences or situations. Two distinct models for this cluster can be identified in the literature of disability studies. First is the medical or functional-limitation model, where attention is focused around what one can or cannot physically or functionally do. This model is closest to the commonsense idea that a disability is what someone has when his or her body or mind does not work properly. The medical model emphasizes body parts that do not function. Labels such as "invalid," "cripple," "spastic," "handicapped," and "retarded" all stem from this model. As we will see later, disability rights advocates note that such terms, originally designating a functional loss, also typically connote a lack of worth.

Two interrelated assumptions constitute the medical model. First, this model sees disability as primarily a medical or biological condition (what we defined earlier as impairment). It claims that the disabled person's functional ability deviates from that of the normal human body. As a result, this model accentuates ways that people with disabilities are dis-abled and are dependent on others for help. Conversely, it designates disabled people as heroic when they participate in what otherwise might be considered ordinary activities such as sports or careers. Second, according to the assumptions of the medical model, if one displays any of a number of physical conditions, one is automatically labeled "disabled." According to this model, it would be nonsensical to suggest that a person who is unable to walk or hear might not be disabled. Key to the medical model is the presumption that disability is a problem that is experienced by an individual (making it a uniquely Western model)[32] as a deviation from an assumed state of normality.

The development of this model can be seen best in the historical relationship between disability and numerous professional and academic disciplines that concentrate upon the management, repair, and maintenance of physical and cognitive capacity. Medicine, rehabilitation, special education, sociology, psychology, and a number of other subspecialties have all, according to David Mitchell and Sharon Snyder, "established their scientific and social credentials (as well as their very professional legitimacy) through the 'humane' study and provision of services to disabled populations that are at the outermost margins of social interest and cultural value."[33] These authors suggest that such service professions have defined and been defined by the experience of disability. In other words, disability is a construction that anchors one end of the continuum between healthy and ill. Disability (which, in this case, includes illness, age, and other diminishments of ability) is an undesirable condition that helps to define the opposite and desired condition of health. Thus, although these professions and disciplines do not focus entirely on disability, their primary emphasis is restoring function and ability, and they aspire to move individuals toward health and nondisability. From these professions, we are shown that disability is a lack or deficit that must be restored by medical or surgical means wherever possible. Medical professionals have the duty of correcting or curing the deficit so as to achieve a state of normality for the individual. When such restoration is not possible, social workers and other service professionals have the job of creating that "state of normality" through help such as personal aids and assistive devices (mainstreaming) or by removing the individual from the normal world altogether (institutionalization).

The perspective of the medical model is that the body is a biological machine that functions to a greater or lesser extent. Disability, then, is located solely within the body, with no appeal to societal or environmental factors. It is an individual rather than societal condition. Under this model, barriers of architecture and attitude do not cause disability, but rather disability is simply a defect of the body. Physical, cognitive, and psychological disabilities may have environmental causes (abuse, physical or emotional trauma, malnutrition, etc.), but cures are available through repair: "treating" bodies through medicine or rehabilitation. According to Christopher Donoghue, the defining characteristic of the medical model is that the state of people with disabilities "is generally considered to be undesirable and, for that reason, they are expected to seek professional assistance to bring relief to their situation."[34] This model rests on notions of deviance, proposing that disability is in conflict with society's morals or values. Erving Goffman and others have successfully demonstrated the ways the "abnormal nature" of people with disabilities serve as a source of stigma among the nondisabled.[35] Building from this, Eliot Freidson proposed that the underlying assumption of rehabilitation is that people with disabilities need to be changed (normalized) in order to become accepted by the nondisabled.[36] The medical model has this principle of normalization at its core, attempting to modify, repair, or relocate individuals with disabilities until they are congruent with societal expectations of normalcy and acceptability.

The medical model falls under great suspicion by the disabled community because of this identification of individual impairments or deficiencies as the source of disability. By imposing definitions of disability based on criteria of deviation from an assumed norm, the model creates clear categories of normal and abnormal. Activists note that it is only a short step from saying that "you have a problem" to believing that "you are a problem." As a result, it is argued that the medical model has contributed to the disenfranchisement of people with disabilities from society. In addition, this model creates impediments to alternative understandings of disability. As long as we define disability as being an issue solely of individual impairment, there is no great need to attend to architectural and attitudinal barriers in society, and little or no obligation for a community to change its exclusive practices toward people with disabilities. For example, the medical definition of disability used in the Americans with Disabilities Act protects people with disabilities only to the extent that their rights of access and employment do not cause "undue hardship" to those from whom they seek relief (employers and businesses, for example). This marks a dramatic difference between disability rights and other civil rights legislation that allows no such exception for discrimination.

The medical model pervades our legal, therapeutic, financial, political, and social worldviews to such a degree that we barely see it as an interpretation. This perspective, with its emphasis on normalization, seems so "normal" to most of us that it is difficult even to think of disability as anything other than a functional loss, which itself creates an impediment as we try to explore alternative perspectives (as will be seen in discussions of theology later in this book). However, when we begin to attend to experiences rather than just to an abstract notion of disability, other options come into focus. Surely impairment, pain, and loss have something to do with many individual and communal experiences of disability. There is, however, something more than just these aspects. Political and social implications, not accounted for by the medical model, are also unavoidable.

Social or Minority Group Model

The second model common to reflection on disability is often called the social or minority group model, in which shared experiences of discrimination and oppression are emphasized. Under this model, individuals are considered disabled insofar as they experience prejudice and exclusion. It is from this perspective that Nancy Eiesland can claim that Jesus himself was disabled, in much the same way James Cone has claimed that Jesus was black—it is the experience of oppression that is central.[37] The minority model begins with the notion that disability is a sociopolitical category. It argues that disability is not so much about what one can or cannot do but rather is about how individuals are treated in their daily lives and by society at large. In other words, "to be disabled means to be discriminated against."[38] Disability under this model is socially constructed and results from society not being organized according to the needs of disabled people. The "problem" is no longer identified as the physical, cognitive, or psychological characteristics of the individual, but rather is identified as prejudicial, exclusive, and oppressive attitudes and barriers—aspects that are related to social or political concerns rather than individual diagnoses. This model highlights the fact that individuals are often more handicapped by the physical and attitudinal barriers in society (e.g., lack of access to employment, education, and health care) than by their own abilities. The recognition of such barriers makes disability into more than just a functional (medical) or theoretical concern—it becomes an issue of justice as well. Built in to this model, then, is a sense that addressing the "problem of disability" means working against unjust social structures and instances of bias and exclusion.

Key to the minority group model is the notion of ableism. Like sexism, racism, and other isms, ableism can be described as "the set of often contradictory stereotypes about people with disabilities that acts as a barrier to keep them from achieving their full potential as equal citizens in society."[39] Among these stereotypes are the beliefs that people with disabilities are inherently unable to manage their own lives, embittered and malevolent, and morally, intellectually, and spiritually inferior to able-bodied people; or, conversely, that people with disabilities are saintlike, cheerful, asexual, childlike, and unusually heroic. Fred Pelka describes ableism as "the belief that people with disabilities are different from 'normal' people, and that their lives are inherently less worthwhile than those of people without disabilities."[40] Under the minority group model, ableism, rather than any physical impairment, becomes the cause and the problem of disability.

In the United States, the development of the minority group model is historically linked to the Independent Living Movement in Berkeley in the late 1960s and early 1970s.[41] At the end of the 1960s, a group of significantly disabled people attending Berkeley (a central locus of other civil rights movements) was attempting to integrate their individual experiences with what they were learning in the university. From their reflections, these people came to see that disability was not so much a matter of impairment as it was one of discrimination; their personal characteristics were not the problem but rather the discriminations they faced within society itself. As a result, they saw that disability, redefined as "social oppression," could be remedied by political activity, lobbying, and direct action. Slogans such as "Nothing about Us without Us" were developed to highlight the political nature of such resistance, articulating the position that "if we have learned one thing from the civil rights movement in the U.S., it's the sense that when others speak for you, you lose."[42] For the first time in the public eye, politically active people with disabilities were proclaiming that they knew what was best for themselves and were presenting "a demand for self-determination and a necessary precedent to liberation."[43]

The recognition of disability as a human rights issue also clarified for disabled people the means necessary for gaining those rights. In addition to protests and public actions, this model accentuated the need for protected minority status, including legal support for civil rights and protection against discrimination. Claims were made that services for disabled people had to be based on the concept of equal opportunity and nondiscrimination rather than on the traditional solutions of segregation and specialization. National and international initiatives were proposed and eventually achieved, including the Americans with Disabilities Act of 1990 and the United Nations declarations of the International Year of Disabled Persons (1981) and the International Day of Disabled People (annually on December 3), all of which focus to some degree on the fundamental human rights of equal opportunity and full participation.

Inadequacies of These Models

Many in both the disability rights movement and disability studies see the minority model as superseding the medical model. In fact, most definitions of the minority model are set up in contrast to the medical model. However, scholars and activists alike are beginning to realize that the minority model itself is not without flaws. One significant concern is that the minority model ignores the very real bodily experience of impairment. By focusing primarily on ableism and experiences of discrimination, the minority model fails to take into account the physical and emotional reality of impairment. When a nondisabled person suddenly becomes disabled as the result of an accident, for example, coming to terms with a newly acquired impairment can create a whole host of emotional and practical difficulties. By emphasizing the social and political nature of disability, the minority model devalues these individual challenges. When the experience of impairment is deproblematized, there is little room for people with disabilities to have a negative or even ambivalent relationship to their impairment. The minority model suggests that all people with disabilities should accept and even embrace their own disabilities/impairments—after all, the impairment is not the (or a) problem. Many people with disabilities, including, for example, those who experience chronic pain, have a much more complex relationship with their disabilities than this model would allow. As Roy McCloughry and Wayne Morris note, "In an attempt to address the fact that the medical model is a deficit model, the social model can go so far as to elevate impairment to a place beyond regret."[44] In the effort to counter the medical model, which focuses primarily on impairment, proponents of the minority model sometimes choose to disregard impairment. In doing so, they disallow a wide variety of lived experiences of disability.

One way activists and scholars have tried to negotiate these two models is to heighten the distinction between disability (as socially created) and impairment (as a physical attribute of the body), thus allowing the medical model to speak to impairment while the minority model addresses disability. In this way a paradigm is established for disabled people in which impairment/disability becomes similar to sex/gender and race/ethnicity. This construct does have advantages for the lived experience of disability, allowing for political activism even when one has an ambivalent relationship with one's own impairment. However, the distinction between disability and impairment becomes dangerous insofar as it can be presented as an unconquerable dualism or dichotomy—one part of which (disability) tends to be valorized and relevant to the public sphere and the other part (impairment) privatized or silenced. In this way, each model "produces and embodies distinctions of value and power."[45] In addition, as Mairian

Corker and Sally French describe, since disability and impairment are discursively related (it is very difficult to "talk" about disability without referring to impairment), "such practice marginalizes the role of discourse in creating and challenging disability oppression."[46] The presupposition that the boundary between disability and impairment is solid does not allow us to explore adequately the experience of disability, because this experience is "in between." This leads Margrit Shildrick to observe that "at best, we have 'leaky bodies and boundaries.' "[47] Trying to work with the medical and minority models in a dichotomous fashion ignores the leakiness of our bodies and misses the full richness of the experience of disability.

In addition, focusing too heavily on either of these constructs leads us to forget, as was noted at the beginning of this chapter, that disability is only one of a number of experiences that contribute to the identity of people with disabilities. These other identity experiences are ignored by both models altogether. Susan Peters describes the shortcoming in this way:

> Until recently, I viewed disability through the lenses of social injustice and societal oppression. I committed myself to a disability rights movement in the United States that demanded unity and strength, derived from collective identities and promoted in the common experiences of oppression. Within the last few years, however, I have felt that something was missing—my sense of self. I began to feel the need to re/define myself as an individual and to validate my personal biography of unique lived experiences in multiple communities— only one of which was my disability network of political affiliations. I began a search for self-identity that is more complex and personalized, and more grounded in sense of physical and psychological self-image than in the political identity that had previously consumed my thoughts and activities.[48]

The medical model emphasizes body parts, ignoring the identity of the whole person and dismissing the role of society or culture in the experience of oppression. The social model emphasizes minority group status, stressing the similarity of people with disabilities without making a place for individual differences, and ignoring the sometimes negative bodily experiences of people with disabilities. Even if we try to hold the two together in tension, we see only categories of impairment and oppression. Both models fail to capture fully what it really means to be a *person* with a disability.

An especially important challenge to both the medical and the minority group models comes from the Deaf community.[49] Many Deaf people do not consider themselves as people with disabilities but rather as members of a linguistic minority.[50] The Deaf argue that their difference is not about function or public perception but is actually a communication difference—they "speak" in sign language rather than English or other aural languages. As a result, they see their situation as radically different from that of people with disabilities. For example, one author points out that the Deaf are not disabled when they are among others who communicate through sign language, "whereas a group of legless people will not transcend their motor impairments when they become part of a legless community."[51] Similarly, being Deaf is not defined by experiences of discrimination or exclusion, or even by a person's ability to hear. People who are Deaf can have a range of hearing abilities from "perfect hearing" to "profoundly deaf"; conversely, there are people with severe or complete hearing loss who do not identify as Deaf and do not participate in the community of Deaf people. The issue of whether Deaf people are a linguistic minority or are disabled (within the context of either the medical or the minority model) has generated intense debate and discomfort among disability rights activists as well as within Deaf communities.

A striking example of the challenge to define deaf/Deaf identity may be seen in the debate over cochlear implants. In the cochlea (a part of the inner ear) of a hearing person, sound waves are translated into nerve signals. Some types of deafness result from sound waves failing to reach the cochlea or from the cochlea failing to make the translation into nerve signals. The cochlear implant (CI) is a piece of technology that helps to compensate for the hearing loss with a bundle of electrodes surgically implanted into the cochlea combined with a body-worn speech processor. Like other medical interventions, this procedure has both benefits and risks. In many cases, the CI provides the recipient with the ability to identify and distinguish a wide variety of sound frequencies, enabling the individual to function with fewer barriers in society at large. From this perspective, the CI is seen to restore what was lost in terms of relationships and experiences as well as auditory function. At the same time, the CI requires extensive auditory therapy, can be painful, and, in most cases, does not restore full hearing but only offers the recipient more cues to help make sense of the Hearing world. Some members of the Deaf community have vigorously challenged the use of these implants, especially in children who are not yet able to make such a decision for themselves, seeing the CI as contributing to a sort of genocide against Deaf Culture.[52] The extreme side of this movement also exerts pressure for deaf people to give up hearing aids—"sort of a Deaf-liberation equivalent to bra-burning"—and resists any attempt to conform or adapt to the expectations of Hearing culture.[53] While this debate touches on many issues, it also highlights the inadequacy of both the medical and minority models to address the experience of the Deaf community, who see their "disability" as neither a medical impairment nor a minority experience (at least not one that has a reason to work politically with other "disabled" groups), but rather as a unique and legitimate cultural form.

Critiques such as these that come from Deaf Culture, along with the awareness of the multiplicity of responses to disability and the multidimensional character of human life, now lead some to question the existing models of disability. For example, Corker and Shakespeare state:

> We believe that existing theories of disability—both radical and mainstream—are no longer adequate. Both the medical model and the social model seek to explain disability universally, and end up creating totalizing, meta-historical narratives that exclude important dimensions of disabled people's lives and of their knowledge. The global experience of disabled people is too complex to be rendered within one unitary model or set of ideas.[54]

The existing models of disability are both totalizing and limited in scope—neither is adequate to fully capture or explain the lived experience of disability. From our contemporary perspective, we can see that both essentialize (either physical attributes/function or social location/minority status) and privilege one group over another (healthy over disabled or oppressed over oppressor). Moreover, the move from modernism to postmodernism shows us that these essential categories are constructions. In this way, we might suggest that "the disabled" is not a natural category but rather is one that has been and continues to be constructed and, thus, can be deconstructed. This is a move that disability studies is only beginning to note. As Branson and Miller write:

> What we are exploring is the discursive construction of a category with shifting referents and shifting significance, a concept that demonstrates *par excellence* that its meaning lies, in Derrida's terms, in "*différance*," in the establishment of meaning through the assertion of difference. No finite meaning is ever achieved, but meaning is constantly deferred as people manipulate it for their own strategic ends. The meaning of "the disabled" is elusive but dramatic, vague in its specificity, and destructive in its application as this label is applied to others and as "the disabled" are defined by difference, with the boundaries of their identify deferred. It is a label that threatens us all but one that is assumed by the majority of the population to be embodied in others.[55]

These authors are among the first to note that the exploration of the concept of disability is at the core of the construction of "normal" subjectivity, part of an attempt to define and understand oneself in relation to the embodied other. This observation, that our understanding of "disability" is in direct relation to any understanding of "normal" or even of "self," makes clear the need to analyze and critique our models and their consequences in thought and action.

The Limits Model

It is my contention that we must attend to both the medical and minority perspectives but also be willing to go beyond them and be open to new models.[56] As we have discovered, the term "disability," as it is commonly used in the two existing models, is too often an absolute category without a level or threshold. One is either disabled or not. As noted earlier, from this perspective "one cannot be a little disabled any more than one can be a little pregnant."[57] Yet reflection on the lived experiences of people who identify as disabled, as well as those who do not, shows the category of disability to be a fluid construction. As discussed previously, ambiguity in my own identity is part of what leaves me dissatisfied with both the medical and minority models. Today, as I sit to write this text, I may feel disabled—aware of the pain and limitations of my body and of the barriers imposed by the physical environment that surrounds me. Tomorrow, sitting comfortably in a chair discussing this work with a friend, I may feel not-disabled. Though this fluidity may not be the primary experience for all people, either with or without disability, most of us experience some situations where we feel more or less disabled than in other situations. Such fluidity reminds us that disability is not just an either/or—it is also a "when," "where," and "how." Lived experiences of disability like these have no home within either the medical or minority models.

Attention to fluidity, as well as to the commitment that disability is as much an identity statement as it is a biological or sociopolitical condition, leads me to a consideration of disability as an instantiation and reminder of human limits. The limits model differs from the medical and minority models in that it does not attempt to divide participants into one of two categories (either disabled or not-disabled) but instead offers a new way to think about what disability is. It attempts to engage in critical reflection on embodied experience and offers us a way to think about the limits of each person and situation and of what such limits may enable or make difficult. Where the medical model begins with an evaluation or assessment of limitations, the limits model begins with the notion of limits as a common, indeed quite unsurprising, aspect of being human. Unlike the minority model, the limits model avoids categorization and instead encourages us to acknowledge a web of related experiences, suggesting, for example, that a legally blind person may in some ways be more similar to a person who wears glasses than to a person who uses a wheelchair. The medical and minority models offer valuable perspectives; the limits model offers a companion piece that emphasizes reflection on the experience of embodiment in its various formations, including disabled embodiment.

Sallie McFague suggests that the test of a model is in looking at what it allows us to see and what it allows us to say, knowing that every model is partial and is only one square in the quilt. We can see and say that the limits model has potential insofar as it highlights the fact that we all experience limits, that these limits differ, and that these limits are accepted, rejected, accentuated, complicated, degraded, and lived in many different ways. It offers us the ability to think of the presence of limits as a natural and good aspect of being human that at the same time is inherently difficult and challenging. It provides us with a new paradigm to make sense of ability and disability. This perspective of limits does not universalize, relativize, or minimize individual experiences but instead proposes an area of common ground in the midst of the recognition of exceptional incarnated and environmental differences. It gives us a place for some very important conversations to begin. It does not dismiss the insights of the medical or minority models but offers a needed theoretical perspective that helps make greater sense of "the experience of disability."

Key to the limits model is the recognition that "disability" is actually more normal than any other state of embodiedness. As such, disability should not be an afterthought to models of embodiment. As Stuart notes, "In truth the human body is only ever temporarily-abled and hence reflection on the disabled body should be central to any theorizing on the body."[58] As a starting point, the limits model notes that good health is never a permanent state, so the "exception" (disability) is perhaps actually more "normal" than the norm (able-bodiedness). Beyond this, however, the limits model highlights the ways and degrees to which we all experience limitation as an unavoidable aspect of humanity. Limits are not an unusual experience and might even be considered an intrinsic element of being human. Some limits are more profound than others, and many are not accommodated by our physical and social environment, but I argue that limits are more common than we typically consider them to be. We must recognize the existence and prevalence of limits and begin with disability or limits as central to our theoretical and theological reflection rather than as exceptions. The limits model proposed in this work attempts to do just that: to start with the human variations of ability as the norm, and to build theory and theology from that starting place.

Beyond offering an important complement to medical and minority models in disability studies, the limits model has a number of direct implications for theological reflection. As we will see in the chapters that follow, the limits model highlights the fact that all people are limited to varying degrees, and offers this perspective as a foundation for theological reflection. When understood as part of what it means to be human, limits are no longer something to be overcome in search of perfection or something that is experienced as a punishment for sinfulness. From the limits perspective, sin might now be redefined as an inappropriate attitude toward limits as we both exaggerate and also reject our own limits and the limits of others. Disability might be understood as limits that are not accommodated by the environment.[59] Rather than minimizing the experiences of disability, this perspective allows us to identify areas where our limits become disabling due to physical or social barriers, relocating sinfulness. It also identifies prejudices we hold about limits—that is, how we see some limits as "natural" (we cannot fly) and others as "defective" (I cannot run)—and offers an opportunity for a critical reexamination of such views. Moving away from such prejudices, we might instead explore the relationship between limits and creativity, or wonder what the existence of limits tells us about the nature of humanity. Through this new lens, questions may also be raised about images and understandings of God.

Christian theology has not, until now, looked at disability from a perspective anything like that of the limits model. When disability has been considered at all, such attention has been based primarily on medical or minority understandings of disability, raising questions such as: Is the reason for my disability my own sin or that of my parents? How might my congregation work to better include people with disabilities in worship? Under these models, disability has rarely been used as a source for theological reflection. In the chapters that follow, we will continue to attend to all three models as we examine our past inheritance and future potential for disability in the Christian tradition. In addition to discovering a long history of attention to disability and other "unusual" forms of embodiment, we will see that the medical, minority, and limits models each has value as a square in the quilt we make as we consider future constructive possibilities for disability and Christian theology.

2

Disability and Christianity

Religious communities have often been unhelpful, and even harmful, in relation to people with disabilities. Stories such as the following are not unusual:

> As a person with a life-long disability, growing up in the church exposed me to a wide range of religious responses to disability. These folk theodicies are summed up in the familiar remarks: "You are special in God's eyes. That's why you were given this disability"; "Don't worry about your pain and suffering now, in heaven you will be made whole"; and "Thank God, it isn't worse." I was told that God gave me a disability to develop my character. But at age six or seven, I was convinced that I had enough character to last a lifetime. My family frequented faith healers with me in tow. I was never healed. People asked about my hidden sins, but they must have been so well hidden that they were misplaced even by me. The religious interpretations of disability that I heard were inadequate to my experience.[1]

Of course no single story can capture the diverse, complex, and enigmatic connection between persons with disabilities and the wide variety of religious communities and practices. But, even limiting our scope to Christian communities, it is not hard to find troubling examples: pastors say that "only the devil within us prevents each and every one of us from immediately acquiring a perfect body";[2]

churches proclaim that "handicapped persons become witnesses for Christ, His healing of bodies a sign of the spiritual healing He brought to all people";[3] book titles such as *Conquering Disability* and *God's Power and Our Weakness* also emphasize this connection.[4] Perhaps worse yet, Christian communities frequently ignore people with disabilities altogether. Even today, barriers of architecture or attitude intentionally or unintentionally exclude people with disabilities from worship services. Many church buildings are still not physically accessible, and even when congregations have made their sanctuaries more accessible, it is often the case that pulpit and altar areas still pose significant barriers. This unwillingness to think all the way through accessibility issues may betray implicit assumptions: for example, that there would be no reason for a person in a wheelchair to need access to the lectern. Beyond issues of architecture, pastors and other worship leaders still perpetuate unrealistic images of people with disabilities as either pitiful or inspirational. Language offensive to people with disabilities (blind to the truth, lame excuse) is used uncritically, as are metaphorical connections between disability and sinfulness (I once was blind, but now I see), leading to what Brett Webb-Mitchell calls "the betrayal of people with disabilities."[5] While many people with disabilities have found welcome in the church, many others still wait outside the gates.[6]

Nancy Eiseland writes, "The persistent thread within the Christian tradition has been that disability denotes an unusual relationship with God and that the person with disabilities is either divinely blessed or damned."[7] As she points out, "Neither represents the ordinary lives and lived realities of most people with disabilities."[8] When people with disabilities have been considered at all, they have historically been looked at as symbols of sin (to be avoided), images of saintliness (to be admired), signs of God's limited power or capriciousness (to be pondered), or personifications of suffering (to be pitied)—very rarely are people with disabilities considered first as *people*. This chapter will explore the relationship, and occasional lack of relationship, between disability and Christian theology in order that we might better understand the roots of our traditions as well as the possibilities through which we might move forward.

The Challenges of Historical Review

There is no doubt that the body is important in Christianity. As Margaret Miles reminds us, "Christianity is the religion of the incarnation."[9] Far from ignoring the body, Christian authors have written about embodiment from the earliest times. While these writings are both numerous and explicit, with few exceptions the historical texts and traditions on embodiment have not been the subject of scholarly review in the contemporary era.[10] Unfortunately, this lack of scholarly interest makes it easy for some to jump too quickly to stereotypically negative assumptions about *the* historical Christian view of the body. Miles notes that contemporary theologies "frequently rest on the assumption that we have received an overwhelmingly negative view of the human body" as our inheritance from the Christian past.[11] Indeed, claims along the lines of "Christianity subordinates the body to the soul" or "Christianity has always preached hatred of the body" are not hard to find. While these "sound bites" may seem to support unambiguous notions of Christianity's negation of the body, such stereotypes are far from accurate.

From the outset, it is important to recognize that even what we mean by "body" may not be what an ancient person, biblical figure, or medieval philosopher had in "mind." As Dale Martin notes, "When we as modern persons read ancient documents, especially the Bible, and come across words like *body* and *soul, spiritual* and *physical,* we naturally take them to mean about what they mean in modern culture."[12] However, as Martin and others demonstrate, these are inaccurate assumptions. As an example, Hector Avalos cites difficulties in the study of the Hebrew term usually translated as "leprosy," a term that "does not have a precise equivalent . . . in modern English or in any modern language because our paradigm and classification of diseases are very different from what they were in biblical times."[13] In addition to changes in definition and meaning, many of the categories that have shaped modern conceptions of the body (like natural/supernatural, physical/spiritual) did not exist in the ancient world as dichotomies, or functioned quite differently in the past than they do for us today. Even conceptions of the material and biological have varied over place and time, as we continue to see today in discussions of the socially constructed nature of embodiment.

As we search for discussions of disability in the Christian past, we must also remember the varied social locations of authors and audiences of the texts we examine. As an example, Amanda Shao Tan reminds us that "using the Bible to discover how Jewish society perceived disability presents some difficulties, since it was not intended to be a book on various disabilities nor an anthology of the lives of disabled people."[14] Quite simply, ancient authors were not concerned with helping us understand their views toward the body, and we must take care to remember this as we read. For example, when we read Augustine talking about the body as a "stinking corpse," we would likely assume from our standpoint that this is a statement about bodies. But Augustine may instead have intended this as a way to stress the importance of the soul, or the irrelevance of the body after death. We can note, for example, that many times an author will use "body" in vastly different ways, sometimes even within the same work, or will express a paradoxical relationship between embracing and overcoming the body.

One final note is that the historical record that has survived is only part of the story. For example, Peter Brown observes that his work on marriage and sexuality comes from the upper-class world; information from the poor and the illiterate has been lost to time.[15] Martha Edwards reminds us that the historical record blurs distinctions and loses particularities, noting that "there were differences, surely, between the experiences of a wealthy Athenian man who had cerebral palsy and the lame daughter of a poor island family. Yet even such a huge distinction is lost [from our evidence], to say nothing of subtle differences."[16] So whenever we search for the historical body, we also need to be aware of things unseen. We cannot simply do a word search for "disability," "impairment," or "health" and assume that such an examination will tell us about the place of the body in Christian history. We must look deeper than this.

The Importance of Historical Review

Clearly, then, reading the body in the history of Christianity is no simple task. Yet we cannot just let the past be past. Historical review is important not only as we seek to understand the past but also as we work to relate it to contemporary challenges and constructions. Delwin Brown defines theology as "the creative reconstruction of inherited symbols, the construction of a tradition's future from the resources of its past."[17] Based on this definition, he describes the theologian's task as follows:

> The theologian—as analyst, critic, and artist—is a tradition's caregiver. Her or his task is to try to discern the varied conceptual possibilities ingredient within a tradition's lived realities, to formulate and elaborate these potentialities, to evaluate them in relation both to the practice of the communities that house them, often unknowingly, and the critiques of the critical discourses that surround them, thus to advocate some conceptual possibilities over others, and finally, to serve as he or she can the integration of these reconstructions back into communal feeling, practice, and articulation.[18]

As we work to discern and elaborate the contributions of the past, Brown argues that the theologian is called to be creative. The theologian is an analyst, critic, and artist, and, to some degree, the past becomes the artist's (as well as the tradition's) raw materials.

According to Brown, this means that "it is not enough to understand and take seriously a particular past or a variety of pasts. . . . we must also ask how canalized pasts become constitutive in present understanding and how present understanding appropriates its pasts. We must ask what pasts are and what they are for."[19] Not only must we pay critical attention to the past in and of itself, but we must also explore, question, and propose how the past might serve or challenge contemporary communities and traditions. As we look at historical understandings of the body, we do so not only to gain information about the past; these inherited images and notions still function in church and society today, and thus we must always keep an eye on the contemporary significance, contributions, or dangers of the images that we explore.

Sheila Greeve Davaney describes this relationship between past and present not only as one where tradition contributes to and can serve as a critique of current understandings and practices but also as one where tradition itself constitutes us. She writes, "Our current context is the product of the vagaries of complex and varied historical processes that have preceded our era and of our own contemporary responses to and transformations of these processes."[20] We are made by history even as we ourselves make history. Recognizing our historicity—our agency as well as locatedness within historical strands of particularity—the task before us is to resist authoritative and essentialist interpretations while still recognizing "how the past constitutes the present in concrete and powerful ways."[21]

As Davaney and Brown show us, the past is still active in the present. Within the Christian tradition, the core sacraments act to remind us that the past is always with us and in us. Christians still use biblical quotations and ancient theological statements and draw on Greek and other premodern assumptions to make sense of modern and postmodern life experiences; these elements are an integral part of the living heritage of Christian communities today. As long as churches read scripture passages and philosophers quote Plato, as long as theologians act as caretakers for a tradition or challenge it to examine its own functionality through conversation with and criticism of its own particular history, and especially as long as we understand ourselves to be constituted to some degree by what has come before, it is important that we return, and return again, to the inherited historical body to explore as best we can what was said and thought, meant and dreamt, and most especially embodied in our historical past.

Historical Foundations

Talking about the body belongs to every discipline. Some of the most exciting new studies on body and embodiment are from sociology, rhetoric, and other areas of the humanities.[22] A review of the body in the religious past could look primarily at non-Christian sources,[23] or it might look explicitly at the history of the concept of disability from ancient to modern times.[24] Examinations of embodiment might begin with Peter Brown and his historical study of sexuality,[25] or with some of the very interesting work in recent years on the dietary practices of women in historical context.[26] Reflection on the body, as has been shown by these authors and others, is open to multiple approaches and perspectives and could be studied productively through a wide variety of lenses.

The history of the body could be traced to the beginning of history itself, as some of the earliest known human records relate to concerns over the body or bodies. Artifacts, hieroglyphics, pictographs, and cuneiform writings of Egyptian, Assyrian, and Persian civilizations demonstrate early religious understandings of illness and healing.[27] Scholars such as Gary Ferngren and Darrel Amundsen have looked at understandings of health and healing in what they term "animistic societies";[28] others such as Henri-Jacques Stiker and Giuseppe Roccatagliata have focused more explicitly on ancient understandings of physical and mental illness.[29] Examinations of health and healing might also be traced to the flourishing of Hippocrates and Asclepius in the fifth century B.C.E.,[30] or to any of a number of other healers or physicians.

Christian understandings of the body clearly rest on our inheritances from Plato and Aristotle and their notions of the relationship between form and matter. For Plato, knowledge cannot be found in the natural world, since knowledge is unchanging and the natural world is a place of constant change. In the *Phaedo,* Socrates asks if the role of the body in knowledge is that of "hinderer or helper" and then responds to his own question by stating that the body is an inaccurate witness, and that thought is best when it has as little to do with the body as possible. Knowledge can only be found in the world of Forms. We see this exemplified in book 7 of the *Republic,* where, in discussing the practice of astronomy, Plato asserts that it does not matter whether a man stares up at the heavens or has his face flat on the ground—he will not learn anything of importance by studying the natural world in that way. The story of the cave in the *Republic* offers a similar lesson. Thus, as Plato states in the *Phaedo,* "He attains to the knowledge of them in their highest purity who goes to each of them with the mind alone . . . he has got rid, as far as he can, of eyes and ears and the whole body."[31] The body and its impulses might not be evil, even though they need to be kept under control (see the analogy of the charioteer),[32] but they will not (and cannot) take us to the world of true Forms.

Plato's teaching was challenged by Aristotle, who was in some ways less dualistic in his thinking. Aristotle dismissed the division of body and soul as pointless, saying, "It is as meaningless as to ask whether the wax and the shape given to it by the stamp are one."[33] For Aristotle, the abstraction of the formal essence of a thing, its universal characteristic, is based on its inclusion in particular things. For example, familiarity with all kinds of trees—with their various shapes, sizes, and colors—allows one to contemplate the idea of the tree, the universal form. While this in some ways avoids Plato's dualism of form and nature, Aristotle's deductive process also leads to a presumption of normality and rejection of the other. Rather than simply describing the material world, his work defines normal and abnormal against each other, with abnormal as not just different but as less (and undesirable). Thus in *Generation of Animals*, Aristotle suggests that, with humans as with animals, any physical difference that "departs from type" (i.e., the able-bodied male) becomes a "monstrosity" that is not only less than ideal but also less than human. Aristotle states that the "first beginning of this deviation is when a female is formed instead of a male," a situation which he also describes as a "deformity."[34] Among the most extreme cases of such deformity are children with birth anomalies. Aristotle states that in these cases a child "has reached such a point that in the end it no longer has the appearance of a human being at all, but that of an animal only."[35]

Thus the Judeo-Christian tradition(s) developed in a world that already had abundant assumptions and interpretations of the body. Plato contributed much of what was further developed by Descartes, the separation of form and matter, body and soul. Aristotle offered a more integrative alternative but simultaneously created the idea of the norm accompanied by a hierarchy of value, which then allowed for the classification of certain people as abnormal, deviant, and deformed. While others in ancient times also had much to say about embodiment—whether they, like some Platonists, disavowed the relevance of the body altogether or, like some in Greek medicine, developed holistic interpretations of health and healing—it is perhaps Plato's division of mind and body and Aristotle's division of normal and abnormal that set up an inescapable groundwork for Christian interpretations of embodiment and difference.

The Hebrew Bible and Bodies

Reading a previous generation of biblical scholars as well as early writings on embodiment theology, one might easily assume that the ancient world had two distinct and completely different conceptions of the body—the Hebrew and the Greek. A common generalization is that ancient Judaism had an overwhelmingly positive attitude toward the body. This claim has some basis in evidence: examination of ancient texts show that there was little rigid dualism between body and soul, and human beings seem to have been regarded as unitary. What this picture ignores is the diversity within ancient Judaism, overlooking the many Jews, like Philo of Alexandria, who held very "Greek" concepts of the body.[36] Additionally, it is not difficult to find examples in ancient Judaism that problematize embodiment. Even a quick reading of Leviticus will show an overwhelming concern with the body, particularly what goes into and comes out of it. As Jon Berquist notes, "The Hebrew Bible obsesses about bodies."[37] It is superficial to assume that ancient Judaism embraced the body (especially nonnormative bodies) or that it had an unambiguous acceptance of physicality.

In his groundbreaking studies of medicine and health care in ancient Israel and early Christianity, Hector Avalos explores notions of body and embodiment in the biblical text.[38] He argues that, while the Hebrew Bible is a necessary point of departure for discussions concerning the health care system of ancient Israel, it is erroneous "to assume that the Hebrew Bible is an accurate depiction of the health care system of Israel in all the instances where biblical texts discuss or provide clues regarding the subject."[39] He notes that political motivations, literary motifs, and hyperbole, among other features of the Hebrew Bible, may mislead us about actual historic conditions. As was highlighted earlier, these texts were not meant to teach modern readers about ancient notions of embodiment. With this caution in mind, we can see from the biblical texts that ancient Israel had a variety of notions about bodies, and that a considerable number of disabilities, both physical and mental, are mentioned in the Bible. Illness and disability were everyday realities that needed to be made sense of in a religious context.

One significant theme found in the Hebrew Bible is that sickness is God's punishment for disobedience. In Deuteronomy, for example, we see descriptions of disease and sickness as God's response to wrongdoing by the people.[40] In Deuteronomy 32:39 the Lord says, "I kill and I make alive; I wound and I heal," showing that while disease and injury may be a consequence of sin, they are clearly also within the realm of God's control. Disease, as a manifestation of God's wrath against sin, can be seen on both an individual level and a national level. For example, Miriam is smitten with leprosy for questioning Moses' special relationship with God.[41] On a wider scale, when David sins by holding a census contrary to God's will, the Lord sends a pestilence to Israel, leading to the death of 70,000 people.[42] Disease can also be sent to the enemies of God's people, as the stories of the Exodus illustrate.

However, disease is much more than just a punishment doled out by God. Throughout the Hebrew Bible we see the promise of health and prosperity for the covenant people if they are faithful to God: "If you will diligently hearken to the voice of the Lord your God, and do that which is right in his eyes, and give heed to his commandments and keep all his statutes, I will put none of the diseases upon you which I put upon the Egyptians; for I am the Lord, your healer."[43] As Berquist notes, "Israel's understanding of the body paralleled its understanding of social reality."[44] The Israelite idea of "health" was complicated by its interactions with notions of purity and impurity. Avalos notes that there were some skin conditions, for example, that might not pose much of a physical danger to patients or render them physically unfit for most tasks, "yet Israelite ideology would view them as 'sick' because there was a visible abnormality, which, even if not regarded as physically dangerous by a modern Western physician, was 'dangerous' in other ways."[45] Impurity, while overlapping with conditions regarded as "illness," was viewed as that aspect of a person that rendered the individual fit or unfit to participate in the community. Avalos notes that such impurity need not be physically visible, and that it sometimes continued to exist even after visible signs of illness disappeared.

The writings in Leviticus generally describe chronic illness as an impurity. In Leviticus 21:16–23 and elsewhere, the sick have restrictions placed on their ability to participate in sacred events and are not considered equal members of the community.[46]

> The Lord spoke to Moses, saying: Speak to Aaron and say: No one of your offspring throughout their generation who has a blemish may approach to offer the food of his God. For no one who has a blemish shall draw near, one who is blind or lame, or one who has a mutilated face or a limb too long, or one who has a broken foot or a broken hand, or a hunchback, or a dwarf, or a man with a blemish in his eyes or an itching disease or scabs or crushed testicles. No descendent of Aaron the priest who has a blemish shall come near to offer the Lord's offerings by fire; since he has a blemish, he shall not come near to offer the food of his God. He may eat the food of his God, of the most holy as well as of the holy. But he shall not come near the curtain or approach the altar, because he has a blemish, that he may not profane my sanctuaries; for I am the Lord; I sanctify them.

Legal uncleanness was attached to the disabled, who could participate in cultic observances ("he may eat the food of his God") but could not serve as priests who made sacrifices. The sanctuary could not be profaned. One had to be without defect in order to approach God's place of residence.[47] It is interesting to note, as with Aristotle, that the sick or disabled held a status similar to that of women, whom menstruation made unclean. As Stiker notes, "It is important to underline that in this fashion disability—of all sorts—is *situated*. It participates in the social division: in the opposition between sacred and profane, it is on the side of the profane. But disability is by no means alone there."[48] All of this reminds us that illness and health as described in the Hebrew Bible ought to be viewed in light of moral, spiritual, and cultic dimensions rather than a matter strictly physical in nature.

We also have learned, from feminist biblical scholars and others, that the Hebrew Bible's portrayal of physicality is not unproblematic.[49] When we look at the contemporary inheritance of these texts, we see that interpretations of the story of Adam and Eve continue to be used as a rationale for limits on the rights of women, and purity guidelines in Leviticus are used as part of the challenge against same-sex unions. It is important to pay attention to critical biblical scholarship as we ask what these ancient texts have to say about disabled bodies, recognizing that the overall message cannot be easily stereotyped as either completely negative or overwhelmingly positive. We have quite a complicated inheritance from these texts, one that must be considered carefully as we bring these stories with us into the contemporary era.

And the Word Became Flesh

While the concerns of the Hebrew Scriptures in relation to bodies, illness, and disability are not abandoned when it comes to the New Testament, the narratives of the Jesus story present a new facet to the relationship between religion and embodiment. As Kallistos Ware notes, "The spiritual value of the human body is firmly underlined by the central event on which the Christian faith is founded: God's flesh-taking or incarnation."[50] In telling the story of the incarnation of God, the Christian Scriptures would seem to have embodiment at their heart. From the moment we are told that Mary has agreed to carry and give birth to a special child, bodies become sites of revelation and redemptive action. People are touched and healed. The dead are raised. Jesus' feet are anointed, he throws over the tables in the temple, his hands and side are pierced. The life and death of Jesus as told in the Gospels are very physical. As Isherwood and Stuart note, "He was not a philosopher simply engaging the minds of people on his wanderings through the land. . . . Here was an incarnate/embodied being."[51] From the point of view of the Gospels, the Christian message focuses on a particular body, the body of Christ, that takes away the sins of the world and brings redemption to the world and to each believer.

The biblical account presents Jesus interacting directly with the sick and diseased, highlighting a radical difference between Jesus and the common attitudes and practices of the time. As Amanda Shao Tan notes, "This was revolutionary behavior and must have been a shock to many people."[52] The Gospel stories show numerous examples of Jesus touching the diseased and the outcast. He is described as talking to blind Bartimaeus, healing the woman with the flow of blood, and touching the leper who asks him for healing.[53] Just as in the Hebrew Bible, the people of Jesus' time who experienced illness and disability were considered ritually and/or morally unclean and were thus prohibited from fully participating in the religious functions of the community. Since people with disabilities were also often poor and had to rely on begging to support themselves, they were regarded with double contempt—as cripples and as poor people. But in the New Testament, just as in the Hebrew Bible, the sick and disabled were not totally excluded from all religious places, nor were they fully ignored. For example, the man with a paralyzed right hand and the hunchback woman were both found in the synagogue, a place for prayer and study.[54] The lame and blind were found in the temple with Jesus after his triumphal entry into Jerusalem.[55] In the scriptural record these bodies existed; there was a place for the sick and disabled, even if that place did not entail full participation in the life of the community.

It is also interesting to note that the biblical accounts do not portray Jesus as attempting to heal everyone in Galilee; Jesus is even described as deliberately withdrawing himself from many who came to him for healing. The stories of healing seem to have been unique and specific to the people he encountered. Hearers from ancient to contemporary times are left with the task of interpreting these healing stories. Perhaps they were offered as proof of Jesus' extraordinary power, or to distinguish his message from that of Jewish law. Perhaps bodily healing was metaphorical for spiritual health, or perhaps it was a pragmatic attempt to win converts. We do not know if physical healing actually happened. We must not look at the healing stories as historical accounts but, regardless of their factuality, remember that what has survived for us today is a message that was crafted for a specific audience with a specific purpose. Clearly, the image of Jesus as an embodied person committed to the practice of healing remains relevant in contemporary theological reflection.

Paul: The Occasional Thorn

Discussion of the physical body in the New Testament moves to a new level when we look at Paul. As John A. T. Robinson writes, "One could say without exaggeration that the concept of the body forms the keystone of Paul's theology. In its closely interconnected meanings, the word *soma* knits together all his great themes."[56] Paul's use of *soma* includes the body of sin and death from which we are delivered, the body of Christ on the cross through which we are saved, the body of the Church into which we are incorporated, and the body of the Eucharist through which we are sustained. Unfortunately, Paul's view of the human body is often interpreted as dualistic, claiming the body to be separate from and inferior to the spirit. Many biblical scholars argue that this is not the case. While Paul's comments about the flesh can be taken as demeaning (particularly in relation to women), they can also be interpreted as observations about the fallible nature of human beings.[57] For Paul, being in the flesh means relying on oneself or the law and not the power of God. When he talks of the body, he is attending not only to the physical but also to the social body. Paul constructs his message about this body for particular rhetorical purposes, and it is easy to take these comments out of context or to have difficulty placing them in a context that makes sense to modern readers. As Calvin Roetzel notes, "Few who know him are neutral about Paul. Some love him; others hate him. And so it has always been."[58]

The term *soma* (body) occurs in the Pauline letters a total of ninety-one times. The bulk of the references to *soma* in the Pauline letters are expressions of the body/member(s) analogy. Paul also employs *soma* to mean the bread received in the Eucharist and for the community of the church, referring to both of these things as "the body of Christ." Nowhere does he make a direct contrast between soul and body, except possibly in 1 Thessalonians 5:23: "May your spirit and soul and body be kept sound and blameless." But even here his intention seems to be simply to describe the completeness of the person. When Paul does choose to assert a contrast, this is not between body (*soma*) and soul (*psyche*) but between flesh (*sarx*) and spirit (*pneuma*).[59] The two sets of terms are by no means interchangeable. Robert Jewett finds that Paul generally uses the word *sarx* to describe those urges for our own personal righteousness that keep us from God. In contrast, *soma* is used to describe the unity of the person and the possibility of relationship between persons.[60] Flesh, in Paul's usage, signifies not any particular body or physical aspect of bodies but rather total humanity (i.e., the soul and body together) insofar as it is separated from God. By the same token, "spirit" designates the human personhood in its entirety (again, body and soul together) when it is living in obedience to God. When he lists the "works of the flesh," he includes things such as "quarrels," "envy," and "party intrigues" that have no special connection to the body.[61] As Paul sees it, the mind can become "fleshly" or "carnal" (Colossians 2:18), just as the body can become "spiritual" (1 Corinthians 15:44).

For Paul, then, embodiment is an essential part of being human, and the body is intimately involved in the process of redemption. The final transformation is participation in the resurrection of Christ, during which the body will undergo a change similar to a seed as it germinates.[62] As Rudolf Bultmann writes, "*Soma* belongs inseparably, constitutively, to human existence. . . . The only human existence there is—even in the sphere of the Spirit—is somatic existence."[63] Emphasizing human existence as bodily, Bultmann notes that Paul never uses *soma* to describe a corpse. Moreover, the body is so integrated into human existence that, Bultmann claims, a human being does not have a *soma*, but rather is *soma*.[64] What believers did with their bodies was therefore an intrinsic part of Christian witness for Paul and one of the most obvious means of distinguishing followers of Christ from others.

Paul's body theology veers between the radical and the conservative as he attempts to work out the implications of salvation in response to real people and situations. He disrupts the reproductive ordering of male and female bodies by recommending celibacy (1 Corinthians 7:32–34) and proclaims the equality of all bodies (Galatians 3:28), but at other times he mimics the gender hierarchies and social-symbolic ordering of bodies found in the priestly writings (1 Corinthians 6:19). In the communities that Paul founded, the body—most especially the body of the young male—was to enjoy none of the carefree moments of indeterminacy allowed it by non-Christians. The body was not a neutral thing; Paul firmly set it in place as a temple of the Holy Spirit. At the same time, Paul was determined that his own state of celibacy should not be adopted by the church of Corinth as a whole. To do so would have been to sweep away the structures of the pious household, an act that might have undermined Paul's own command. In his attitude toward marriage as in his tolerant attitude toward the eating of "polluted" foods, Paul sided with well-to-do householders who had the most to lose from separating from the non-Christian world, perhaps in part because it was these householders who supported his mission to the gentiles most effectively.[65] Paul's understanding was pragmatic as well as theological, often a subject of discussion and never unimportant to his ministry.

An interesting aspect to Paul's understanding of bodies can be seen in the discussion of his "thorn in the flesh." 2 Corinthians 12:6–10 reads:

> But if I wish to boast, I will not be a fool, for I will be speaking the truth. But I refrain from it, so that no one may think better of me than what is seen in me or heard from me, even considering the exceptional character of the revelations. Therefore, to keep me from being too elated, a thorn was given me in the flesh, a messenger of Satan to torment me, to keep me from being too elated. Three times I appealed to the Lord about this, that it would leave me, but he said to me, "My grace is sufficient for you, for power is made perfect in weakness." So, I will boast all the more gladly of my weaknesses, so that the power of Christ may dwell in me. Therefore I am content with weaknesses, insults, hardships, persecutions, and calamities for the sake of Christ; for whenever I am weak, then I am strong.

What Paul meant by this "thorn" has been a subject of intense debate from the days of the early church and still is a subject of dispute today. The earliest view, held by the Latin fathers as well as some modern proponents, understood the phrase to refer to a physical disorder.[66] For example, Tertullian believed Paul's thorn was a pain in the apostle's head or ear. Other possibilities that have been discussed include epilepsy, hysteria, depression, headaches, leprosy, malaria, and even stuttering.[67] A modern interpreter, T. J. Leary, suggests that the thorn may have been a visual impairment, citing Galatians 6:11 that Paul's handwriting was larger than his scribe's, and 2 Timothy 4:13, where Paul talked about parchment notebooks being easier to use than wax tablets for those with poor sight.[68] Other interpreters question the physical disorder interpretation, wondering whether anyone like Paul, who traveled so widely around and across the Mediterranean, could have done so while he was experiencing overwhelming physical problems.[69]

An alternate interpretation suggests that the thorn was persecution. For example, Chrysostom took the thorn to represent Paul's opponents.[70] Jerry McCant argues that the thorn in the flesh was not a physical malady but referred to certain persons, most likely Christians in the Corinthian church.[71] Yet another interpretative tradition claims that the thorn was Satan or sin, a perspective accentuated in the Middle Ages when the thorn was associated with sensual temptations or spiritual trial, a perspective supported by the Vulgate rendering of "thorn in the flesh" as *stimulus carnis*. More recent versions of this view see the disturbance to be spiritual torment caused by demonic visitations or the pricking of the apostle's arrogance.[72]

The precise identity of this thorn has eluded interpreters for centuries, and this question, ultimately, is not resolvable. The strongest hypotheses involve some sort of human enemy or physical ailment. Either way, the affliction bore directly on Paul's stature and authority before the Corinthians, and so had social consequences within the Corinthian community. If the thorn was a human opponent known to the Corinthians, then the challenge to Paul's authority was direct and obvious. If the thorn was a physical affliction, then the Corinthians may have been concerned that Paul was unable to heal himself. As Susan Garrett notes, "Whatever the identity of the thorn, the cross/resurrection paradigm governs Paul's reading of the divine response, for Christ's resurrection had shown 'power made perfect in weakness' (2 Corinthians 12:9) to be God's characteristic design for Christian life."[73]

As is clear even from this brief review, Paul's teachings about the body were more complex than they might at first seem, and contain much more than just the idea that the body is separate from and inferior to the spirit. We see in Paul someone who was struggling with how to craft a message that would be meaningful to the people of his time and relevant to a newly forming church. His use of body language to describe the Christian community has great potential

for embodiment theologies. Of course, what Paul had to say is not entirely positive, especially as we look at the theological relevance of the human body. At
the same time, though, the ability to make clearer sense of the complexity and
contextuality of even these aspects of Paul's message is useful as we examine
his legacy in church communities today. In addition, Paul's discussion of the
thorn might be valuable as we explore the theological relevance of the human
experience of limitation, an example we will return to in later chapters as we
discuss foundations for a theology of limits.

From Past to Present

The tension that is evident in Paul over the nature and value of the human body
has been played out in various ways throughout the history of Christianity.
From both the Hebrew Bible and the New Testament stories, there was the possibility for "a very earthy, fleshy, physical way to connect with one's God," which
could have set the pattern for a positive approach to the body.[74] By the end of
its first century, however, Christianity shared the unease about the body apparent in surrounding societies. Some early Christian thinkers proposed that the
incarnation was a necessary evil—God endured incarnation to enable humanity to achieve the desirable state of *dis*incarnation—and others, who could not
accept even that, wondered if Christ had not just *appeared* to be enfleshed.[75] In
the midst of these early philosophical debates, it is also interesting to note that
the ideas of health care reflected in early Christianity were an important factor in attracting converts and may have contributed to the rise of Christianity
itself.[76] Thus ambivalence toward the body—including the different or disabled
body—is found not only in the scriptural tradition but also in the early positions and practices of Christianity itself.

As early Christianity became institutionalized, so too did the conviction
that the human body was something to be overcome, or at least ignored, especially in the doing of theology. Tertullian, Irenaeus, Clement, Augustine,
and many others offer us great sound bites regarding the devaluation of the
body (although their individual positions on embodiment are often far more
complex than this). By the Middle Ages, the Gregorian reform, Scholasticism,
and other aspects of religious and intellectual life (especially notions of pen-
ance and hell) emphasized this move toward spiritualization; simultaneously,
however, medieval spirituality—especially female spirituality—was particularly
bodily.[77] Similarly, while the Protestant Reformation could be described as a
retreat from embodiedness to inwardness, we also see a challenge to traditional
notions of virginity and sexuality (highlighted in the dismissal of demands of
celibacy for clergy). From Descartes's work on the relationship between mind

and body to the Romantics' attention to beauty and sensory experience, the role and value of the body has scarcely escaped attention. As we move to look at interpretations of embodiment in the contemporary age, we cannot forget the long and complex inheritance that serves (as Delwin Brown reminded us earlier) as our raw material for new theological construction even as it continues to function in expected and surprising ways through the continuities and discontinuities of tradition.

Disability and Contemporary Theological Reflection

No matter how well we describe Christianity as a religion of the body, the actual history of attitudes toward the disabled body is complex and, in most cases, does not occasion optimism. As Stuart notes, "It is one of the paradoxes of the Christian scriptures and tradition that disabled people are everywhere and nowhere at the same time."[78] Christian interpretations of disability have run the gamut from portraying disability as a symbol of sin to being an occasion for supererogation. These interpretive images appear throughout religious language, scripture, worship, religious education, leadership, and all aspects of Christian life.[79] Disability is interpreted as punishment for one's own sin or for the sin of one's parents, a test of faith, an opportunity to build character or to inspire others, an occasion for the power of God to be made manifest, a sign that one lacks faith, or simply a mysterious result of God's will.[80] Language exemplifies these notions: people with disabilities are often called saints, angels, courageous, blessed, or special witnesses to God. Scripture is used to reinforce these ideas, whether it valorizes weakness (2 Corinthians 12:9), reveals disability as an opportunity for God's self-revelation (John 9:3), or implies that there is a special place in God's kingdom for the disabled (Luke 14:16–24). Unfortunately, these interpretations too often mean that when people with disabilities have been considered at all by religious communities, they have been looked at as objects to be avoided, admired, pondered, or pitied—very rarely have people with disabilities been considered first as people. In addition to contributing to a model of God as a great puppeteer who controls and determines everything, including (but not limited to) experiences of disability, these explanations lack recognition of (and even deny) the personhood of the person with the disability.

One particularly ingrained image is that of God as divine Father and human (especially a disabled human) as child. Jennie Weiss Block discusses the implications of viewing a person with a disability as "an eternal child." She writes, "This creates a situation where reasonable developmental demands are not made and the individuals are not held accountable for their actions."[81] She suggests that this "also promotes treating a person as if they were a child in an adult body, which denies the person's sexuality and can lead to inappropriate behavior."[82] As an example, she notes that adults with disabilities speak of being spoken to and treated like babies or children. In religious terms, this model can lead to a person with a disability being viewed "as a holy innocent, without sin, incapable of any wrongdoing, saved by virtue of their disability."[83] For example, she notes that people with developmental disabilities are told in some religious communities they do not need the sacraments because they are already going to heaven. Feminist theologians and others have raised many of the problematic implications of Father and child language, but it is important to add to these critiques an analysis of the ways in which this image contributes to the characterization of people with disabilities as children with limited agency. Under this model, the person with a disability is assumed to lack capability, responsibility, culpability, and almost any sort of "ability"—assumptions that carry significant theological weight. The Father and child model, like the medical model, ignores individual and corporate agency and often implies limited access to responsibilities and power. The power/control Father image is theologically suspect not only in terms of God's identity but also for what it then necessarily implies about human identity and ability or disability.

For some who have rejected the Father and other anthropomorphic power/control images of God, the question of why there is disability instead receives this contemporary liberal answer: God does not cause disability. It is not God's fault. Perhaps God put the laws of nature into motion and then stepped back. Perhaps disability is just part of the way the universe works. As we will see in the next chapter, Sallie McFague is an example of a contemporary theologian who appeals to randomness to explain the existence of disability and other related experiences. For many people with disabilities, the randomness explanation makes more sense than to imagine an old man in the sky who decides certain people should experience life with a disability. Yet there are significant concerns that come with this appeal to randomness. First, given societal interpretations of normalcy, there tends to be an implicit notion not only that a person's disability is random but also that it is a random aberration (a negative value is placed on this instantiation of randomness). Second, the explanation of randomness is not applied evenly: disability is seen as random, but ability often is not, at least within the context of theological reflection. In addition to not going far enough to challenge negative assumptions of the past or to take sufficient account of the diversity of actual human embodiedness, the randomness response can also be a theological cop-out. While some theological and philosophical approaches do reflect on random or chance occurrences, others take a lack of causality as meaning the situation is no longer interesting for reflection. We ought not say "God does not cause disability" and leave it at that. Experiences of disability, and of all human particularity, can be valuable data for theological reflection.

Rather than dismissing the experience of disability as part of the uninteresting randomness of life, we ought to instead reflect upon what the existence of disability, as well as the unique experiences of particular individuals with disabilities, can show us about our theological claims and constructions. Attending to the three different models of disability described in the first chapter, the next three chapters will explore ways in which we might reflect on disability as a meaningful source for theological reflection.

3

Theology and the Disabled Body

Perhaps the most fundamental insight of the medical model is the simple observation that bodies are different from each other. Within the framework of this model, such an observation typically is combined with a value judgment: some bodies do not function as well as other bodies, and it is best to be as close as possible to an ideal body (beautiful, fit, thin, able). Embodied difference is an unsurprising observation—by looking around our world, we can see differences between bodies and can consider how our own bodies have changed over time. Any particular Olympic athlete can do things that I cannot do, I can do things that my grandmother cannot do, and, as a contemporary country song expresses, "I ain't as good as I once was." What is surprising is that theology has not attended to these differences. Of course, it has at times remarked on or reinforced categorized differences between men and women, various ethnic groups, parents and nonparents, and so on, but scarce attention has been paid to the fluidity within and between individual bodies.

Cornel West notes that such attention is key to what he calls the new cultural politics of difference. He writes: "Distinctive features of the new cultural politics of difference are to trash the monolithic and homogeneous in the name of diversity, multiplicity, and heterogeneity; to reject the abstract, general, and universal in light of the concrete, specific, and particular; and to historicize, contextualize, and pluralize by highlighting the contingent, provisional, variable, tentative, shifting, and changing."[1] This emphasis on multiplicity and particularity proposes a marked departure from much of modern thought, which has often relied on assumptions of universality. We see the beginnings of this move with the advent of feminist and liberation theologies as they have proposed alternatives to traditional antimaterialism within Christian theology. Postmodernism has also offered a significant challenge to earlier universalizing perspectives on the body (and on other elements of social life), the effects of which are beginning to be felt throughout Christian theology.[2] Process theology, as well as other theological movements, has also emphasized this move to the particular and concrete. As scholars have taken up the challenge to pay attention to real bodies and confront dualistic tendencies, local perspectives have been highlighted as legitimate sources for theological reflection and construction. Yet even in this move to recognize difference, the full range of human experiences often has been overlooked. This becomes especially clear as we attend to disability. As we shall see, even feminist and postmodern scholars who deliberately focus on the body tend to assume that a healthy body is normative. Still lacking until now is a perspective that critically reflects on the full range of human experiences of embodiment, including disability, as primary source material for theological reflection and construction.

The move to attend to local perspectives, including the particularity of embodiment, can be seen quite clearly in feminist theology. Beginning with Valerie Saiving's groundbreaking article, "The Human Situation: A Feminine View," significant questions have been raised about universal claims in theology.[3] These concerns are named most bluntly in Mary Daly's famous convention: "If God is male, then the male is God."[4] By using jarring phrases such as the "sisterhood of man," Daly demonstrates that terms and theologies are not universal and all-inclusive, and, as a result, necessitate what she terms "a castrating of language."[5] Similarly, Rosemary Radford Ruether suggests that we cannot yet answer the question "Can a male savior save women?" because the "full humanity of women is not fully known."[6] As she explains,

> The uniqueness of feminist theology lies not in its use of the criterion of experience but rather in its use of *women's* experience, which has been almost entirely shut out of theological reflection in the past. The use of women's experience in feminist theology, therefore, explodes as a critical force, exposing classical theology, including its codified traditions, as based on *male* experience rather than on universal human experience.[7]

Similar challenges to the falsehood of so-called universal claims are made in other liberation theologies. In his argument for the blackness of Jesus, James Cone argues that white academic theologians "fail to recognize that other people also have thought about God and have something significant to say about Jesus' presence in the world."[8] Similarly, Gustavo Gutiérrez demands, based on the experiences of the "oppressed and exploited land of Latin America," that theologians "reconsider the great themes of the Christian life within this radically changed perspective and with regard to the new questions posed by this commitment."[9] Daly, Ruether, Cone, and Gutiérrez are early examples of theologians who challenged the viability of universal theologies and argued that experiences of difference must be recognized for reasons of justice as well as theological adequacy.[10] This challenge has continued within womanist, *mujerista*, native, queer, and other liberationist movements, where local perspectives have increasingly been highlighted as legitimate sources for theological reflection and construction.

However, as demonstrated quite clearly by the title of the book *All the Women Are White, All the Blacks Are Men, But Some of Us Are Brave*, each new voice has also witnessed continuing universalizing tendencies.[11] In each movement, some local perspectives are highlighted, but others are ignored, "whitewashed," or "straightened out." Even in the deliberate attempt to recognize difference, the full range of human experience is overlooked too often. This becomes clear especially from the perspective of disability: even within theological movements where we would expect to see particular and intentional inclusion of the diversity of bodies, disability has been strangely absent. Disability is rarely mentioned within theologies that otherwise attend to identity particularities (e.g., even as feminist theology and queer theology have attended explicitly to the body, especially in relation to sexuality, they rarely address diversity of ability or embodiment), and disability itself has not yet emerged as a theological lens (e.g., there has not yet been a fully articulated feminist disability theology).[12] There is a surprising absence of disability as a topic in academic and professional journals.[13] Textbooks and readers on religion and theology routinely fail to mention, let alone reflect on, experiences of disability.[14] Other works mention disability only in passing, as part of a list of other diversities, but fail to treat these issues as relevant for theoretical or theological construction. Even cutting-edge work on gender, race, and sexuality still assumes a generically healthy body to be normative. Disability is invisible, even within theologies interested in embodiment.

As we look for possible ways to include disability reflection into the realm of theology, one approach is to continue to push existing theological models to attend to and include this level of diversity. Just as African American women challenged white feminists to include them in "feminist theology," those who identify with disability can also raise our voices and challenge other movements and theologies to be more inclusive. We see this happening in a few loci within theology; similar inclusion has been seen recently in other disciplines such as educational theory.[15] In addition to this essential pursuit of recognition and inclusion, we must also ask a deeper question: What would it mean to take the body (in all its diversity and fluidity) seriously in constructive theology?

Embodiment Theology

Embodiment theology offers a constructive and deliberate alternative to the lack of attention paid to genuine embodiment in traditional theological reflection and construction. At its core, embodiment theology is about a change in perspective, a "decentering and recentering," according to Sallie McFague.[16] It begins with the notion that we live embodied lives, and that there are no exceptions. James Nelson, one of the first to use the term "body theology," writes a descriptive account of this perspective: "Body theology starts with the fleshly experience of life—with our hungers and our passions, our bodily aliveness and deadness, with the smell of coffee, with the homeless and the hungry we see on our streets, with the warm touch of a friend, with bodies violated and torn apart in war, with the scent of a honeysuckle or the soft sting of autumn air on the cheek."[17] Nelson emphasizes the real, concrete, sensory everyday experiences and particularities of the human embodied experience. He describes the theology that grows from this as "nothing more, nothing less than our attempts to reflect on body experience as revelatory of God."[18]

Embodiment theology, as it has developed since Nelson's early work, is more than a reflective or evocative pastime. Beginning as it does with the extreme particularity of embodied experience, body theology proposes a unique challenge to universal claims and assumptions. As it has grown out of liberation concerns related to gender and sexuality, the political as well as the experiential is highlighted. As Lisa Isherwood writes, "Working through the body is a way of ensuring that theories do not get written on the bodies of 'others' who then become marginalized and objects of control."[19] Attention is paid to issues of power and naming, to the political as well as the personal. Embodiment theology is concerned with all that is written on, of, or by the body, going far beyond sensory experiences to include science, politics, economics, media, and many other concerns of postmodern life.

As we approach the topic of embodiment and theological reflection, John Dunnill reminds us of an important caveat:

> Anyone who is now reading this must be an embodied being. How else could you be reading? Since what I want to write about is the

body, it is important to acknowledge at the outset that being bodies is a condition we all share. It may be obvious, but that very obviousness is significant: we take it for granted because we have all been bodies for so long. We have together a mass of experience of being bodily, and that ought to mean something. Yet we do not often think about what it means to be bodily. In fact thinking about it at all is a bit embarrassing. We avoid the subject, on the whole, unless circumstances force it on us, as when we are ill. It seems we are constitutionally uneasy about being bodily.[20]

Embodiment theologies begin by noting that we have not taken our bodies seriously in doing theology. They assert that we not only *have* but *are* bodies, and that when we reflect theologically we inevitably do it as embodied selves. In a way, then, theologies have always been embodied because all theologies have been explored and lived by people with bodies. Our bodies make our reflections possible; they also influence our theological perspectives. Through our particular bodies, each of us knows the world in particular and unique ways, and this knowledge influences our theological reflections. The role of our bodies (in fact, the necessity of our bodies) must be acknowledged as an unavoidable part of theology. Embodiment theologies begin with a conscious focus on these issues, taking reflection on embodied experience seriously as a critical source for the doing of theology.

Reflection on experiences of embodiment challenges, and in fact subverts, the notion that we can engage theological topics from a detached, intellectual (i.e., disembodied) position. In some arenas, this claim is a familiar one. From the early work of Ruether and Daly to contemporary writings in feminist, liberation, womanist, *mujerista*, queer, and other theologies of difference, the argument is credibly made that gender, race, orientation, and so on do make a difference in our theological reflections as well as the ways in which we move through the world. Even in the move from understanding difference as essential to seeing it as historically constructed, academia is comfortable with the claim that these particularities—these aspects of embodiment—make a difference (even if it is still an object of debate as to what these differences might be as well as from where they come). We are not, however, accustomed to thinking about these issues in terms of other aspects of embodiment. What difference, for example, do labels such as able/disabled, young/old, strong/weak, or athletic/ couch potato make? Are experiences of pain, illness, or limitation relevant? Does a cold or arthritis or cancer affect theological reflection? Should they?

Body theology, as with reflection on the body in other disciplines, is now beginning the important project of engaging bodily differences and exploring how these varied embodiments might contribute to our understandings and interpretations of the world. This can be seen most clearly in recent attention to theology and fitness,[21] bioethics,[22] pain,[23] and sexuality.[24]

McFague's Contribution

Sallie McFague is one of the few theologians who has made a specific effort to develop a systematic theology based on notions that emerge from the standpoint of embodiment. She provides us with one of the most complete and influential examples of the shift to recognize local perspectives in a way that avoids many (though not all) of the universalizing tendencies of her predecessors. In particular, her model of the world as the body of God provides a valuable way for us to thoughtfully consider the natures of and relationships between the world (human and nonhuman) and God. For McFague, this profound embodiment leads to an environmental ethic where we are called to treat the earth as if it were the literal body of God, caring for the environment much as we would care for a friend or even for God directly. However, she notes that the claim that the world is God's body can lead to other insights or questions as well, inviting us to join her in this project. As we shall see, McFague's model does more than offer us a framework for a Christian theology that can be open to reflection on the fluidity and diversity of embodiment; I also suggest that theological reflection on disability can strengthen McFague's own argument in a manner consistent with her overall approach to God and bodies.

Building on her early work on metaphorical theology, McFague has committed her academic life to developing and analyzing models of God that seem most appropriate for our day, searching for those that best fit her criteria of coherence with both the Christian tradition and the scientific worldview. With an understanding that all religious language is metaphorical, she argues that theologians are charged with the task of finding and using the "the best images available to us in order to say something about the divine."[25] To elaborate, she explains:

> The choice of theological models is neither arbitrary nor absolute; models are selected and survive because they make sense out of human experience. Certainly, they are required to "fit" with our experiences of God, but their range, since they deal with the divine-human relationship in its many implications, goes far beyond any narrow view of that relationship. Major theological models are not

merely "religious" but encompass all dimensions of life in the world. Thus, we must demand, if we are to reject a "ghetto Christianity," that these models also fit with and illuminate all ways of looking at the world and all "truths" about life we hold to be significant.[26]

This concern with "good" models and metaphors permeates McFague's later work. She proposes pragmatic criteria, suggesting that we must look at whether specific images lead to helpful or harmful results.[27] She rejects traditional patriarchal and imperialist images of God, seeing them as opposed to the continuation and fulfillment of life, and she gives examples of nuclear annihilation and women's oppression as destructive outcomes of these traditional models. This leads her to the work for which she is perhaps best known, her proposal of the metaphors of God as mother, lover, and friend.[28]

For McFague, our choice of models ought not be arbitrary, and so she offers four criteria for "good" models: continuity with the basic Christian paradigm, commensurability with postmodern science, a concern for the well-being of our planet, and consideration of actual embodied experience.[29] The first criterion, continuity with the basic Christian paradigm, is important to her because this is what locates her work within Christian theology (rather than an alternate religious tradition or worldview).[30] The second, commensurability with postmodern science, is important for McFague because she argues that "just as theology has always understood its central beliefs in terms of the picture of reality in different times, so reflective Christians today are also called to the task of understanding their faith in light of the current picture of reality."[31] She sees this not only as an issue of credibility but also as one of pragmatic concern—the scientific worldview tells us things that we need to hear and understand for the future well-being of the world.[32] The third criterion, concern with planetary well-being, is also a pragmatic one in that it recognizes that (from McFague's perspective) religion is irrelevant if we destroy our planetary home. Finally, her concern with embodied experience draws upon her understanding of epistemology—her belief that knowledge comes mediated through bodies. Thus, for McFague, a model or metaphor is "good" insofar as it coheres with these four criteria, and especially insofar as it leads to pragmatically good outcomes.[33]

McFague's book *The Body of God* attempts a systematic theology based upon the model of the world as God's body, a model briefly mentioned in her earlier work and one that she has come to see as particularly valuable due to its nonanthropological emphasis. In this book, she attempts "to look at everything through one lens, the model of the universe or world as God's body. . . . using the lens this model provides, we ask what we see and what we can say about various dimensions of the relationship of God and the world."[34] As with other embodiment theologies, she highlights stories that describe the God-human-world relationship as located in and interpreted by bodily experience. She argues that all relationships are between bodies, including the relationship between human beings (or the nonhuman world) and God. Thus her main goal in this book is to lead the reader to "think and act as if bodies matter."[35] McFague suggests that this is especially appropriate within Christianity, which she calls "the religion of the incarnation par excellence."[36] Noting such central themes as the incarnation, resurrection, and the church as the body of Christ, McFague argues that Christianity is and always has been a religion of the body. As such, she sees it as especially relevant that Christian theology return to a consideration of the role that particular embodied experience plays in religious thought and practice. In addition, as with her prior work, she believes that the model of the world as the body of God is one that is perhaps the "most good" (given her earlier criterion) for this time and place. We will return to her specific claims from this book later.

It is important to note at this point that McFague intends her model of the world as the body of God to be just that—a model. She writes that it "represents one square in the quilt, one voice in the conversation, one angle of vision."[37] The model of the universe as God's body does not see nor does it allow us to say everything, and it is not meant to replace all other models. It is, from her perspective, a particularly good model because it is in line with the view of reality coming to us from contemporary science and because it is in line with what she identifies as key Christian stories and teachings. As noted earlier, McFague also argues that this model is especially important and even indispensable based on the state of the world today. She writes that this model "is certainly not the only context within which we need to understand ourselves, our world, and God, but it is a necessary one . . . an offering that Christianity can make to the planetary agenda of our time, the agenda that calls for all religions, nations, professions, and people to reconstruct their lives and their work to help our earth survive and prosper."[38] In other words, she suggests that the model of the body of God is "only one model, but one that is neglected, essential, illuminating, and helpful both to Christian doctrinal reformulation and to planetary well-being."[39]

McFague's construction is particularly helpful in the way that she develops an entire systematic model around the notion of embodiment. She gives us the clearest interpretation and description to date of embodiment theology, including sources, methodology, systematic criteria, and implications. As we look at the critical and constructive possibilities for embodiment theology, McFague offers a good starting point.

Defining Characteristics of the Body of God

McFague's model of the world as the body of God has both epistemological and ontological implications. First, she argues that we must recognize that it is embodied creatures, not disembodied ones, who do theology. Knowledge is necessarily related to the experience of embodiment. We encounter, reflect upon, and understand the world as bodies, not as disembodied minds or souls. As a result, she demands that any authentic theology begin with an awareness of our own bodies and the bodies of others. She calls this "attention epistemology." Taking this perspective as a primary interpretive lens, she asks us to think about what it would mean, for instance, to understand

> sin as the refusal to share the basic necessities of survival with other bodies? To see Jesus of Nazareth as paradigmatic of God's love for bodies? To interpret creation as all the myriad forms of matter bodied forth from God and empowered with the breath of life, the spirit of God? To consider ourselves as inspirited bodies profoundly interrelated with all other such bodies and yet having the special distinction of shared responsibility with God for the well-being of our planet? Such a focus causes us to see differently, to see dimensions of the relation of God and the world that we have not seen before.[40]

McFague's position is that, however else we might believe we have knowledge of God (or of anything else), this knowledge is at the very least mediated through our bodies, if not grounded in embodiment altogether. For McFague, "whatever more or other we may be, we *are* bodies, made up of the same stuff as all other life-forms on our planet."[41] Any knowledge that we have of God, or any understanding we have at all, comes through and is impacted by particular experiences in particular bodies.

The second key aspect of McFague's theology relates to ontology: she claims that the world *is* God's body. McFague's notion of God is panentheistic—she does not reduce God to being equivalent to the world, but she does place the world very directly in God, noting that "everything that is, is in God and God is in all things and yet God is not identical with the universe."[42] Or, stated more simply, "God is incarnated in the world."[43] Even more striking for this project is McFague's claim that "the body of God is not *a* body, but all the different, peculiar, particular bodies about us."[44] McFague uses this claim as the foundation for her environmental ethic, where the entire world around us (human and nonhuman) participates in ("is") the body of God. However, she notes that this claim can lead to other questions and insights as well. McFague does not raise the issue of disability in her work, but it is easy to move from discussion of "peculiar, particular bodies" into theological reflection on human experiences of disability.

McFague's model proposes specific characteristics of God based on her criteria of coherence with the Christian tradition and the scientific worldview. These criteria lead her to reject the traditional monarchical model of God as Lord and King, which she sees as especially dangerous. Citing Gordon Kaufman, she describes this as a pattern of "asymmetrical dualism" in which the world and God are only distantly related, and all power and responsibility reside in God.[45] The monarchical model also suggests that God is apart from and other than the world. McFague argues that while this model has a strong psychological pull (making us feel good about God and about ourselves), its characteristics are inappropriate for a model of God in light of our current world situation. She names three major flaws: "God is distant from the world, relates only to the human world, and controls that world through domination and benevolence."[46] These "flaws" lead to logical conclusions: it is of no importance what one does in and for the world because it is not the king's "primary residence," the natural world is unimportant in relation to the human world, and humans have no power to make productive changes. The direct result of this model of God, according to McFague and presented in her "Lament for the Planet," is that Christians have become the enemy of the planet and the perpetrators of the ecological crisis (as well as many other forms of oppression).[47]

McFague's concern, then, is with a model of God that "at least should do less harm."[48] Her model does not allow God to be apart from the world but instead "radicalizes both divine immanence (God is the breath of each and every creature) and divine transcendence (God is the energy empowering the entire universe)."[49] She sees this as a particularly relevant model for our time because it encourages us, in her words, "to focus on the neighborhood."[50] The image of power that is present in this model is one of mutual flourishing rather than power over or power from outside, and is based on the basic recognition that the whole (including God) will not flourish unless the parts are thriving. McFague sees examples of this power in the Christian stories of Jesus. She reads John 1:14, "And the Word became flesh and lived among us," as an affirmation of the physical availability of God's presence and of God's affirmation of embodiment. Bodies are not contrary or opposed to God; rather, it is God's nature to be embodied. She creatively retells the stories of Jesus' healing and eating practices, focusing attention on bodily pain and bodily relief. For McFague, these stories prove that the body of God includes everyone, particularly those who have been excluded. Similarly, the incarnation shows that God both values and participates in bodily reality. The emphasis on mutual flourishing through interrelated embodiment is the defining characteristic of God in this model.

McFague's model also has specific implications for our understanding of anthropology. It follows from her description of the "common creation story" that she is concerned that we accurately recognize where humans fit into the scheme of things. This involves an awareness of both place and space—the earth is our home (our place), but it is the home of other beings as well (not simply our space). According to McFague, awareness of both place and space leads to

> a focus on gratitude for the gift of life rather than a longing for eternal life; an end to dualistic hierarchies, including human beings over nature; an appreciation for the individuality of all things rather than the glorification of human individualism; a sense of the radical interrelatedness and interdependence of all that exists; the accept- ance of responsibility for other forms of life and the ecosystem, as guardians and partners of the planet; the acknowledgment that salva- tion is physical as well as spiritual and hence, that sharing the basics of existence is a necessity; and, finally, the recognition that sin is the refusal to stay in our proper place.[51]

For McFague, and for others in the Christian tradition, sin is living a lie: it is the refusal to accept our place and our proper limits so that others, human and nonhuman alike, can have the space they need to survive. We live this lie, she says, in relation to other human beings, to other animals, and to nature itself. By looking at who we are in the picture of contemporary science, we see that we are, on one level, mundane, of this world, and radically interrelated. On another level, we see that we have power and responsibility, and both the abil- ity to destroy the world and to help creation continue. Humanity, she says, is "profoundly responsible."[52] She believes that the story of space and place fits especially well with the Christian story, embracing humanity's role as God's partner in creation.

McFague suggests that the model of the world as the body of God has implications for all of the traditional themes in theology. In addition to her clear emphasis on notions of God, Jesus, humanity, and sin, she believes that her model is Trinitarian, preserving both the radical immanence and the radi- cal transcendence of the divine. McFague has a very clear notion of salvation that includes the natural world. She writes, "Creation as the place of salvation means that the health and well-being of all creatures and parts of creation is what salvation is all about—it is God's place and our place, the one and only place. . . . Salvation is for all of creation."[53] The church, for her, is both a sign of this new understanding and one of the responsible parties in its development: "a critical social body helping to bring about the new reality."[54] She defines ethics most clearly in her later books as thinking and acting in ways that are consonant with this model and beneficial to all creation.

It is important to note that McFague's model not only reflects and interprets traditional Christian themes but also is influenced by other theological commitments. She does not rely solely on a scientific or ecological interpretation of the metaphor. Her commitments are seen most clearly in her call for solidarity with the oppressed, a nebulous proposal if based only on observation of the natural world. At a basic utilitarian level, we see that all of creation is interdependent, and that one life depends on many others in order to survive; however, the natural world often looks like it is more about the strong overcoming the weak than solidarity with the oppressed. One wonders what solidarity might even mean for a tree or an ocean. Moving beyond the common creation story and the testimony of nature, McFague appeals to what she calls the "scandal of Christianity," demanding that humans engage in solidarity with the outsiders, the outcasts, and the vulnerable.[55] She admits that this is beyond the initial scope of her model, writing that "neither biological nor cultural evolution includes this radical next step of identification with the vulnerable and needy through the death of the self."[56] However, she does not see this commitment as completely opposed to the evolutionary model: "Solidarity with the oppressed, then, becomes the Christian form of both consonance with and defiance of the evolutionary principle. It is consonant with it because it claims that there is a next stage of evolution on our planet. . .it is defiant of it because it suggests that the principle needed for this to occur is not natural selection or the survival of the fittest, but the solidarity of each with all."[57] McFague's commitment to what she calls the "Christian paradigm" demands that the model of the body of God be interactive and go beyond the simple application of the metaphor to engage with other sources as well. As we apply the model, she suggests that we gain an understanding of God by examining and interpreting bodily experience, both human and nonhuman. At the same time, we understand our own place and role in the cosmos by drawing on other sources for knowledge of God, which for her include the Christian stories of Jesus.

Evaluating McFague's Model

As was noted earlier, McFague offers four criteria for theological adequacy: continuity with the basic Christian paradigm, commensurability with postmodern science, a concern for the well-being of our planet, and consideration of actual embodied experience. It can be argued, and in fact has been by McFague herself, that her model fails (at least to some extent) in each of the four criteria. Some have wondered how well her model can actually fit within Christianity, claiming that she does not take sufficient account of traditional images of God or of the uniqueness of the story of Jesus.[58] Others note that her readings of Christian history and her conception of the "Christian paradigm" are at times simplistic or creative at best, suggesting that she "misrepresents the theological tradition."[59] Some challenge her scientific interpretations, noting that she proposes more unity and coherence to the world than might be allowed by postmodern science.[60] Critics also wonder whether her approach to planetary well-being is appropriate, whether it makes sense to erase all differences between the human and nonhuman world, and whether we should love all of nature.[61] In fact, in *Life Abundant*, she herself questions whether this model can contribute in any way to planetary survival.[62] A few critics have suggested that McFague's criteria lead us toward "a cultural and moral relativism" because they emphasize only what is best for our time, leaving no clear guidelines for future evaluation or suggesting any intrinsic value to nature or other aspects of this model.[63] Another common criticism is that these criteria necessarily limit the scope of her project, emphasizing only middle-class Christians living in the postindustrial world and failing to draw on other religious or cultural resources.[64] Both her choice of criteria and her application of them have received extensive critical review.[65]

In the midst of all this discussion, McFague's adherence to her fourth criterion, consideration of actual embodied experience, has received scarce critical attention. A few commentators have wondered whether reflection on human experience is an appropriate theological starting point for McFague.[66] Others have looked at her epistemological commitments more generally, particularly her reliance on embodied experience.[67] However, none have analyzed or challenged the sorts of experiences she takes into account as sources for knowledge of God or for evaluation of the model. McFague argues that one of the criteria by which we should evaluate a model is the degree to which it makes sense of actual embodied experience. Thus it is my argument that an appropriate test of McFague's model of the world as the body of God is to examine it from the perspective of disability. As we shall see, McFague's analysis is incomplete insofar as it overlooks the full diversity of human (as well as nonhuman) embodied experiences and overlooks the theological insights that may be gained from reflection on these differences.

McFague's Model and Reflection on Disability

At one level, McFague's work would seem to be well suited for theological reflection on experiences of disability. Her model focuses our attention on significant epistemological and ontological issues related to God and bodies, asking how our particular bodies affect what we know (about ourselves and about God) and how our particular bodies affect what is (including divine and human nature). It is perhaps the most ambitious model to date to reflect on embodied experience as foundational for theology. This model is an especially relevant starting point when we look at human experiences of disability because it gives us a way to incorporate embodied experiences into our theological reflection and construction. By applying her model to a wide variety of theological issues, McFague demonstrates how such a starting point can ripple throughout the traditional concerns of theology—including the nature of God, interpretations of the stories of Jesus, understandings of sin and salvation, and foundations for ethics—and can offer implications for religious practice.

In contrast to the frequent disregard and disdain for the body found in Cartesian idealism, Platonism, Neoplatonism, and contemporary deconstruction, McFague's model of the common creation story starts instead "with the mundanity of embodiment and the peculiar forms of unity and differentiation characteristic of that story."[68] She suggests that

> this perspective would support, though of course not demand, a view
> of meaning and truth that takes seriously the diversity of embodied
> sites from which human beings make such claims: the sites that take
> into account race, class, gender, sexual orientation, handicapping
> situations, and so forth. Since there is no one universal, ideal embod-
> iment but many, diverse forms of it, truth and meaning for human
> beings must begin from these embodied locations.[69]

McFague seems very aware that there is not and ought not be any single ideal for embodiment, and that embodiment appropriately takes a wide variety of forms. For her, this is part of the nature of the world, as well as the body of God. She claims this powerfully in her statement that "the particular, concrete, situated *differences* among human beings, who at the same time exist together within the body of the planet, must be starting points for knowing and doing, for embodiment is radically particular."[70] According to McFague's own model, it is the diversity of experiences of embodiment, including, for example, experiences of disability, that must ground reflection and practice.

Unfortunately, McFague herself fails to follow her own claims to their fullest implications. Her application in The Body of God and elsewhere is inconsistent with her notions of what embodiment is all about. Instead of attending consistently to diversity, she herself exhibits idealizing tendencies. This lack of coherence with her own criteria of attention to embodied experiences takes three main forms. First, in many of her mentions of the human experience, she seems to assume a healthy or, at least, "generic" body to be normative. She rarely talks about human bodies as if they contain varied and specific differences but treats them as if they were all the same. Second, she fails to reflect critically on the diversity of the human embodied experience, including the experience of disability. As will be argued later, such reflection could in fact have supported and enhanced her project, but for the most part she ignores such differences. Finally, when McFague does address experiences of difference, she minimizes these as being simply part of the randomness of life and seemingly unimportant for theological reflection. While these events may be and, within her model, most likely are attributable to randomness, the failure to reflect upon what can be learned from these experiences leaves us theologically impoverished and is inconsistent with her practice in relation to other "random" occurrences. By normalizing, ignoring, and dismissing human particularity, she fails to draw on theological possibilities that would contribute to her own project.

For a reader who is sensitive to issues of disability, it is striking that McFague tends to discuss the human body as if it were the same in all its instantiations. She does not pay much attention to experiences of difference. This makes some sense in light of her specific project, which is to emphasize our relation to and responsibility for the nonhuman world. In the introduction to *The Body of God*, she notes that this work "cannot give the needed concrete, detailed attention to such complex issues as racial and sexual discrimination, physical violence, sexual abuse, or compulsory heterosexuality."[71] The project of her work is not to attend to human differences, and she is aware of this limitation. Yet it is still surprising that she talks about "the human body" as if it were one uncomplicated thing. Some of this is quite innocent and appears in the way she uses the term "we" in a way that universalizes rather than acknowledges differences in experience. Her generalizing can also be seen in the actions that she proposes in response to her model: that we should be more sensitive to our use of space, that we should be more aware of the other, that we need to better attend to issues of justice. As was noted in chapter 1, people with disabilities often have a perspective from the underside, a place from which these comments would be inappropriate or irrelevant. In such examples, McFague's use of the word "we" is not accessible to many people with disabilities. Even her notion of the body as a relevant starting point for reflection on God ignores the often complex and ambivalent relationship that we have with bodies: as Anne Clifford notes, McFague neglects "the fact that the body of every concrete earthly being eventually dies and decays."[72]

Related to her lack of attention to the diversity of human embodiment, McFague fails to reflect specifically on the experience(s) of disability. Again, this is not entirely surprising given her commitments and overall goal. Hers is "one square in the quilt, one voice in the conversation, one angle of vision."[73] She does not claim that her model is comprehensive. Yet, because the notion of body is so central to her work, it is surprising that she does not look more closely at specific instantiations of embodiment, such as experiences of disability, before suggesting that we image God as a body or bodies. When she discusses reinterpretations of Jesus, conceptions of sin and salvation, or the role of the church, she does not reflect on or take into account diversity of embodiment, human or otherwise, even though such reflection has the potential to contribute to her proposal. If reflection on bodies tells us something about the nature of God, according to her epistemology and criteria for adequacy, it is then a shortcoming of her project that she fails to attend to experiences of disability. Her model would have been enriched by such attention, particularly in the ways that reflection on experiences of disability offers new constructive possibilities, insights, and perspectives on anthropology and on the relevance of particular models of God.

Finally, when McFague does address experiences of difference, she minimizes these as being simply part of the randomness of life and seemingly unimportant for theological reflection. Her notion that diversity is random does, in some ways, fit appropriately with the ecological model. She writes, for example, that "my life, your life, all life, is a chance happening; so also are birth defects, cancer cells, and AIDS."[74] This is, to a degree, consistent with scientific understandings of evolution and natural selection, although even scientists might question her use of the word "chance," since evolution, though not necessarily purposeful, is more reasonable in some ways than pure chance allows.[75] McFague's failure comes when she refuses to reflect on these experiences and dismisses them as a product of chance. She appropriately rejects theodicies that are based on anthropological models of God, as these are inconsistent with her model. For example, she denies that events such as birth defects or AIDS are caused by God in order to test an individual or to demonstrate God's power or will. She states what these experiences must *not* mean according to her model, but does not reflect on what they may or do mean, or what insight they may give to understandings or constructions of self or God. For example, when she mentions a woman killed in an accident or a baby born with birth defects, she states that "God is not the cause of these events and cannot be if we take seriously the contemporary scientific picture of reality, but God is with us in the consequences."[76] Her response, which she claims relies upon the scientific worldview, is to say that experiences such as these are just part of the whole of life and are something to be accepted as such. God is with us in those experiences. God suffers with us. That is all she has to say.

Rather than overlooking or dismissing particularity as part of the random-ness of life, McFague's model ought to lead us to a perspective that takes par-ticularity as a significant datum for theological reflection. Following McFague's claim that "the body of God is not *a* body, but all the different, peculiar, par-ticular bodies about us," we are turned toward important questions such as: What are the implications of this model if we say that the body of God includes disabled bodies, or can be conceived of as being disabled itself? What is that nature of God if we understand the world, including the presence of disability and difference, to be God's body? How do specific answers to these questions affect church, faith, and community? These questions, as I have suggested, are prompted by McFague's model but are not addressed in her work.

The Disabled Body of God

It is my argument that, rather than dismissing the experience of disability as part of the uninteresting randomness of life, we ought instead to reflect upon what the existence of disability, as well as the experiences of individuals with disabilities, can show us about our theological claims and formulations. Dis-ability (as well as nondisability) may be part of the randomness of life, but failing to recognize and reflect on difference as an important aspect of the metaphor of the body of God leaves us theologically impoverished. Ignoring disability not only hinders our possibilities for reflecting on the fact that the full range of human embodiedness includes experiences of disability; it also causes us to fail to reflect appropriately on the real lived experiences of "nondis-ability." This failure leads us to uncritically accept an assumption that most of us are "normal," that disability and other related experiences are "abnormal," and that "normal" perspectives are central and have theological priority. When McFague or others talk about embodiment, then, we are pushed to think more specifically about the epistemological and ontological implications of theologi-cal reflection from particular bodies, recognizing that we are not all the same, but neither are we completely different from one another.

Awareness of the theological relevance of experiences of disability can work to strengthen McFague's own approach. It continues her work of expanding our resources for theological reflection and responsibility: in addition to paying attention to what the nonhuman world has to teach us about God and commu-nity, it increases our possibilities for reflection on actual human experience. If we learn about God through our bodies, we will learn more about God when we listen to what is known from the variety of types and forms of human bod-ies. This offers the theological community access to previously overlooked and underappreciated perspectives and experiences, attention to which, according to McFague's model, acts to increase our resources for knowledge of God. For example, we might ask why some human limits are accepted or accommodated by society while others are not—questions that can help identify exclusionary practices leading to situations of alienation. Questions raised by this perspective are consistent with McFague's reading of salvation as a situation where every being has its appropriate place. Attention to the diversity of human embodiment makes McFague's model of the world as the body of God into one that is more authentic to her overall purpose as well as more relevant to the particular experiences of people with disabilities.

McFague's model holds within it key foundations for a Christian theology that draws upon understandings of disability. It is appealing insofar as it takes bodies as central and gives us a valuable framework for taking seriously the claim that disabled bodies are a part of creation. It includes concerns for access (space and place) and for interdependence (through the common creation stories), and allows embodied experience to inform our notions of God (the world as the body of God). McFague's model consciously avoids many of the difficulties of the traditional power/control notions of God, which have often been damaging for people with disabilities, suggesting what she calls a decentering and recentering: "We are decentered as the only subjects of the king and recentered as those responsible for both knowing the common creation story and helping it to flourish."[77] Putting McFague's work in conversation with disability, this chapter will conclude with a discussion of disability as a source for such recentered theological construction and will suggest some of the questions, issues, and constructions relevant to such a task.

Key to McFague's anthropology is her discussion of sin, which she defines as the refusal to accept our place, particularly "our unwillingness to stay in our place, to accept our proper limits so that other individuals of our species as well as other species can also have needed space."[78] For her, neither sin nor salvation is an otherworldly matter. Given the model of the world as the body of God, sin against material bodies (people, animals, nature) *is* sin against God.[79] She identifies three forms of sinfulness based on this model. The first she labels "Us versus Us: living a lie in relation to other human beings." She suggests that this form of sin is rather obvious and is epitomized in the disparity between billionaires and the homeless. Quite simply, it means "living contrary to reality, pretending that all the space or the best space belongs to some so that they can live in lavish comfort and affluence, while others are denied even the barest necessities for physical existence."[80] The second form of sinfulness is one she labels "Us versus Them: living a lie in relation to other animals." According to this form, we as humans forget the interrelationship and interdependence of all living things, as well as the distinctive individuality and differences between creatures.[81] The third form of sinfulness, according to McFague, is "Us versus It: living a lie in relation to nature." She describes this form as a lack of awareness of "both our responsibility for nature and our profound and complex unity with it that is the heart of the appropriate, indeed necessary, sensibility that we need to develop."[82]

Reflection on disability clearly resonates with the first lie or form of sinfulness, Us versus Us, especially for people with disabilities who are denied agency and experience economic oppression.[83] I propose that the combination of disability and McFague's model also suggests a fourth lie or form of sin, which might be termed "Me versus Myself: living a lie in relation to oneself." This lie recognizes that we tend to hold inaccurate self-representations, especially insofar as we deny or depreciate our own limits. This is closely related to traditional notions of sin that would have been familiar to McFague, including the proposal by Reinhold Niebuhr and others that sin is either thinking too highly of ourselves (pride, ignoring our own limits) or too lowly of ourselves (sensuality, defining ourselves solely based on our limits).[84] Lying about limits allows us to construct the categories of we and they, of able and disabled. This lie conditions us to believe that wearing glasses is normal but using a hearing aid is not (unless one is "old"), convinces us that it is a disability not to walk but normal not to fly, and highlights adaptive technology "for the disabled" while blinding us (pun intended) to technological aids that are designed to adapt to other situations (e.g., a spacesuit, which may be the ultimate prosthesis). The lie that comes from a rejection of our own limits may at first be one of perception, but, just as McFague argues with the other lies, it eventually leads to the perpetration of injustices that cause harm to self and other beings and that impact the health and even survival of the body of God. This lie directly contributes to both physical and emotional self-harm, as research on eating disorders, for example, clearly demonstrates.[85] It also causes harm to others, through the construction of the illusory categories of we versus they. In addition, this lie contributes to mind-body dualism, placing us at the top of the imaginary intellectual ladder, a position that McFague notes is responsible for many other injustices of space and place that follow.

Awareness of this fourth lie and recognition that limits are a natural and inherent part of humanity could have extended the scope and impact of McFague's project. Reflection on disability supports McFague's notions of space and place, especially within the purview of the social or minority model, which is especially concerned with issues of injustice (or, following McFague, appropriately shared space) for people with disabilities. Questions of access are particularly relevant within McFague's concerns about space, which can in turn

highlight the issue of whether and under what conditions people with disabilities are allowed to enter and participate in public spaces. The lens of disability
also supports McFague's claim that this world is our place, and that we ought
not appeal to otherworldly salvation or images of a detached and solely tran-
scendent God—appeals that have been particularly harmful to people with disabilities. As a whole, McFague's concern with embodiment as a starting place
for theology is very much in line with what we might seek when we look at
humanity through the lens of disability or limits. However, as McFague herself
argues at the beginning of *Super, Natural Christians*, "People only look alike
when you cannot be bothered to look at them closely."[86] Perhaps because of her
overarching commitment to ecological justice, McFague fails in her project to
look closely at diverse people or to consider human embodied differences as
a significant datum for theological reflection. Attending to these differences
could have contributed important theoretical complexity to McFague's model.
Instead, she seems to rely primarily on understandings of humanity gained
from the scientific worldview (which, as critics of the medical model note, is
itself a value-laden perspective). Especially insofar as McFague is interested in
a discussion of human responsibility, including space and place, it is problematic that her model neither is based on the analysis of diverse bodies nor sends
us back to diverse bodies at the outcome of her analysis.

McFague's model of God is especially appropriate as a foundation for a theology of disability because it includes consideration of bodies, emphasizes relationality, demands subject-subject interactions, is panentheistic, understands
notions of God to be metaphorical, and offers itself as only (but importantly)
one square in the quilt. In addition to McFague's concern with bodies, we also
see in her work a demand for the recognition of interdependence: we all "matter" and are connected through the common creation story. McFague is also
clear that her proposal is metaphorical, which reminds us that God is not just
this one thing that we say, and allows an openness to other models and metaphors. A metaphorical understanding acknowledges that there is a diversity of
experiences and interpretations that can be offered by people of various physical and intellectual states, and allows for some of the metaphors of God that
will be presented in the next chapter. Additionally, a metaphorical understanding seems especially appropriate as we attempt to capture the diversity that is
represented in human embodiment. Our multiple bodies suggest that it might
be appropriate to consider multiple avenues toward reflection on God or matters of ultimate concern. Metaphors offer us a significant way to reflect upon
the full diversity of individual situations and responses to experiences of limits,
and so a metaphorical approach may well be the most promising method for
engagement between disability and theological reflection.

McFague's model for God begins with a concern for bodies, including all of the different, particular, peculiar bodies around us. It connects with both religion and science not only as sources of legitimacy but as productive conversation partners that keep us open to new ideas and proposals that might emerge. The image of the world as the body of God is not meant for universal application, but it has a wide range of relevance, and not just for use by people with one bodily experience or with one political concern. Given these attributes, I suggest that, while it is valuable for disability studies to imagine God freely and creatively, there is also benefit to be gained from dialogue with models such as McFague's that are currently being explored within the discipline of theology. In particular, it is my claim that ongoing conversation between existing theological models and those who reflect on experiences of disability is productive and can be mutually beneficial, strengthening and offering new possibilities for both. McFague is one clear example of a helpful model of God that allows (and even embraces) the human experience of diverse embodiment. Her model shows us one constructive possibility for disability and Christian theology, beginning with the medical model's observation that bodies are diverse, are fluid, and differ in ability. Our next chapter will explore a second option: Drawing upon the commitments of the minority model, how might we imagine a liberation theology of disability?

4

Liberation Theologies of Disability

Even as attention to disability highlights fundamental issues about the diversity of human embodiment, it simultaneously raises significant justice concerns. From a theological perspective, we can see parallels between this lens and the commitments of various liberation theologies. According to James Cone, a liberation perspective means seeing Christian theology as "a rational study of the being of God in the world in light of the existential situation of an oppressed community, relating the forces of liberation to the essence of the gospel, which is Jesus Christ."[1] Or, in the words of Gustavo Gutiérrez, liberation theology "is a theological reflection born of the experience of shared efforts to abolish the current unjust situation and to build a different society, freer and more human."[2] Thus, if we begin with the minority model's observation that people with disabilities experience exclusion and injustice, it seems fitting to study God and church in relation to the situation of this oppressed community and to reflect theologically out of this struggle for liberation. Following Cone and Gutiérrez, we are invited to participate in a disability theology of liberation.

Consideration of disability in Christian communities, deeply influenced by certain elements of the medical model, has often fallen primarily within the realm of pastoral care (how do we take care of people with disabilities, support their families, and address issues of suffering and healing) and, for the most part, has been neglected in theological reflection and within the daily life of religious communities. When church members are asked about disability issues in their congregation, most will respond with a discussion of ways they have learned to respond to individual impairments, usually through changes in architecture or assistive technology. Ramps, elevators, sound systems, and the phrase "please stand as you are able" are seen as fulfilling church obligations to people with disabilities. Disability activists observe that "today most denominations and many local congregations realize that church facilities should be constructed or altered to encourage the presence of persons with disabilities. Yet little effort has been made to promote the full participation of people with disabilities in the life of the church."[3] The history of Christianity's practice in relation to people with disabilities is at best an ambiguous one.

While advances have been made, it is important to recognize that in many Christian denominations discrimination against people with disabilities is not infrequent. Because religious organizations successfully lobbied for exemption from the Americans with Disabilities Act (ADA), churches are still responding on a case-by-case basis to accessibility requests.[4] This means that accommodations that have become standard in other places (stores, banks, schools, etc.) are still lacking in many churches. Religious organizations are "simply out of step"[5] with other organizations, leading some to observe that access for people with disabilities has become for churches "a matter of benevolence and goodwill, rather than a prerequisite for equality and the foundation on which the church as a model of justice must rest."[6] Rather than being a structure for empowerment, religious organizations have more often supported the societal structures and attitudes that have treated people with disabilities as objects of pity and paternalism. Relations between disability activists and religious groups became strained during the ADA lobbying process and have scarcely improved in subsequent years. This leads Eiesland and others to note that "for many disabled persons the church has been a 'city on a hill'—physically inaccessible and socially inhospitable."[7] These barriers of attitudes towards welcoming acceptance—whether real or perceived—may prove to be greater obstacles than staircases ever were.

Another barrier appears as people with disabilities seek access to the pulpit. People with disabilities are often discouraged from seeking ordained ministry or pursuing advanced theological education. Many seminaries contain barriers of architecture and attitude similar to those found in churches; overcoming these barriers is not just a matter of having a ramp to the front entrance but of being fully and multiply hospitable to the experience of a disabled student. The ordination of persons with disability has also been fraught with challenges from a variety of directions. Biblically and ecclesiastically, religious organizations have challenged the right of persons with disabilities to seek ordination. Leviticus 21:18–20, barring anyone "blind or lame, or one who has a mutilated face or a limb too long, or one who has a broken foot or a broken hand, or a

hunchback, or a dwarf, or a man with a blemish in his sight," has been used
to justify exclusion of people with physical disabilities from ordained ministry.[8] Today, in place of overt prohibition, many denominational officers subtly
question the practicality of ordained ministry for people with disabilities. They
emphasize such issues as challenges in fulfilling pastoral duties, problems
in finding appropriate placement, and congregational acceptance. While the
number of ordained persons with disabilities is slowly rising, the number of
ministers, priests, rabbis, and employees of religious institutions who have disabilities remains small.[9] Additionally, students with disabilities who do have
the opportunity for theological education often have been steered away from reflection on disability and encouraged to engage in "serious" scholarship rather
than "personal" concerns.[10] This exclusion from theological reflection is yet
another example of discrimination against those who are differently abled, one
that simultaneously limits the church's own resources for leadership and theological construction around issues of disability.

It is interesting to note that there are few, if any, congregations that do not
include members with a variety of overt and hidden disabilities. In pragmatic
terms, "anyone who is preparing to be a teacher, preacher, pastor, or counselor
in congregations today needs to understand and be sensitive to the experience
of persons with disabilities."[11] Beyond this, understanding more deeply the
experience of a person with a disability not only helps sensitize a minister—
particularly one who is relatively able-bodied—to the experiences of a significant number of people in any given community but also can provide her or him
with a new perspective on what it means to be a human being and a child of
God. Yet instead of drawing upon the gifts of diversity, churches have allowed
barriers to access, participation, and leadership to remain, thus treating people
with disabilities, to use Harold Wilke's term, as "sickened-class citizens."[12]

Christian churches have failed to engage honestly with people who have
disabilities, to seek out and listen to their stories, and instead tend only to speak
to or about them or do things for them. If they are not ignored altogether, people with disabilities have been talked to or about by religious organizations,
but not included as key partners in the conversations. This negligence is also
found in theology. Without ignoring or minimizing the significant emphasis
that has been placed on the inclusion of people with disabilities in recent years,
scholars note that "with few exceptions, the theological community is unaware
of the radical new vision of disability emerging in this country."[13] Lacking an
awareness of anything other than the medical model and physical issues of accessibility, theology has failed, for the most part, to engage the emerging field
of disability studies either as a topic for examination or as a partner in conversation and theological reflection.[14]

Similarly, the field of disability studies has paid scarce attention to religion and has been largely silent on the issue of God. A review of anthologies, introductory texts, and works on methodology shows little, if any, mention of God. A superlative example of this is seen in the *Handbook of Disability Studies*, a landmark work that was designed "to organize and formalize the emerging field of disability studies" and to draw together "the best and most current thinking in the field, the major works and intellectual forces that define the field, the critical issues and problems that persist in the field."[15] In the introduction to this work, the editors state, "While one book cannot include every theory and perspective, a serious attempt was made to reflect the diversity and depth of disability studies in this volume."[16] Given this claim, it is surprising that, in the more than 700 pages that follow, religion is barely mentioned and then only in relation to the institutional history of disability. There is no discussion, even in footnotes, about disability within the disciplines of theology or religious studies, or of any contributions these fields might make to disability studies. This is especially notable insofar as almost all other traditional academic disciplines are represented at some point in the work. Also lacking is any mention of how people with disabilities are present in or absent from religious institutions, which is surprising, since the volume surveys a wide spectrum of other institutional and communal aspects of disabled life. Religion is examined only as a historical influence, with no attention (in this text and most others) to contemporary religious issues or communities, no mention of God, and no consideration that theological reflection might have a contribution to make as one of the intellectual forces that define the field of disability studies.

The silence of disability studies on religion in general is problematic on a number of levels. Given the dominant Christian environment within which the movement operates in the United States, this failure ignores a significant facet of the lives of many people with disabilities. Nancy Eiesland describes the failure of disability studies to address religion in this way:

> For a long time, I experienced a significant rift between my activism and my faith. My activism filled me with a passion for social change that would acknowledge our full value as human beings. But my theological and spiritual questions remained unanswered: What is the meaning of my disability? The movement offered me opportunities to work for change that were unavailable in the church, but my faith gave a spiritual fulfillment that I could not find in the movement.[17]

The silence of disability studies on issues of religious significance distances the field from the real-life values and commitments of many people with disabilities, ignoring that God may have meaning (whether positive, negative, or ambiguous) in the lives of many people with disabilities. By failing to address issues of significance in the lives of the people it speaks for and with, disability studies falls short of its own commitments to inclusivity and relevance. Additionally, it is my argument that this silence has problematic implications for the stability of the field itself. This chapter will argue that it is important for disability studies to attend to images of God for two crucial reasons. First, given the nature of religious belief, destructive notions of God will most likely persist if left unchallenged and will have the potential to sabotage the progress of other aspects of the disability movement. Second, with appropriate reconstruction, alternative images of God have the potential to make significant contributions to ongoing processes of resymbolization and reinterpretation of the experience(s) of disability, an undertaking that is vital for the future of the field.

It is important to note that religion, particularly Christianity, has frequently been cited as a source of destructive stereotypes about people with disabilities. Traditional understandings of God validate detrimental explanations for and analyses of disability. Models of omnipotence support images of dis-ability, and models that fail to challenge such assumptions implicitly perpetuate them. In particular, the traditional image of God as the all-powerful Father enables interpretations of people with disabilities as childlike and lacking agency, allowing for a variety of stereotypic interpretations of disability.[18] Ignoring these images does not make them go away. Thus, when we examine the interaction of religion and disability, it is essential that we look not only at institutional and individual discrimination but also at the religious values, ideas, and images that permeate our webs of meaning. Disability scholars ought to be concerned with religion not just because churches are or can be oppressive institutions but also because personal and societal understandings of disability are saturated with meaning, including religious meaning.

As Naomi Goldberg notes, "Images of God dictate who will feel worthy in society and who will feel inferior, who will be respected and who will be despised, who will get easy access to the literal material goods of culture and who will have to fight for those same goods."[19] Traditional anthropomorphic images of God make God look more like the able-bodied than like the disabled, which puts people with disabilities on the inferior and despised side of Goldberg's balance. Traditional images of God may, for some people with disabilities, be the best way of capturing the relationship between God and disability. Experiences of disability cross all religious, political, cultural, and regional lines—there is no single or typical reaction to the experience of disability, which, combined with other identity factors, means that there will be no single image of God that is relevant or appropriate for all people (or even all Christians) with disabilities.

Some will reject God outright, and others will find meaning in traditional images. However, it is the argument of many people with disabilities, especially those who have rejected the medical model of disability, that traditional and contemporary images of God are biased toward able-bodiedness and perfection, thus reinforcing negative stereotypes toward people with disabilities. For example, John Hull suggests that we think of God as being above average: "The human image of God is usually thought of as the image of the perfectly normal human, but raised to an even higher level of perfection."[20] These images act to deny or dismiss the agency of people with disabilities, insofar as the nondisabled are more like God, and leave traditional (negative) definitions and expectations of disability unchallenged. These images also fail to embrace the fluidity and diversity of individual experiences of ability and disability, leaving us theologically impoverished.

Traditional models offer very little space for a positive valuation of disability, and therefore leave few theological resources for those who embrace disability as a natural part of life. As was argued earlier, concerns with justice demand that traditional models be challenged, especially in terms of the implications these models have in the real lives of people with disabilities. There must be more as well: we need theological resources that allow us to reflect upon the full diversity of human embodiment. Eiesland suggests the following as our starting point: "The challenge for people of faith is first to acknowledge our complicity with the inhumane views and treatment of people with disabilities, and second, to uncover the hidden, affirming resources in the tradition and make them available for contemporary reflection, finding new models of the church in which full participation is a sign of God's presence."[21] As we look at meaningful images of God for people with disabilities, we need to consider immediate concerns with justice, as well as models that will be meaningful for the long haul, both for people who are defined as disabled and for all of us in our own experiences of limits.

What God for Disability?

As noted earlier, disability studies as a whole has paid little attention to religion at all, let alone to images of God. Even for those specifically interested in religion, the emphasis has been limited to questions of access for people with disabilities, particularly with regard to worship, theological education, and ordination.[22] Very little consideration has been paid to reflection on disability as it impacts theological notions. Yet current theological options seem to be inadequate for many, if not most, people with disabilities. While some work has been done to highlight images that are exclusive or oppressive to people with disabilities, very little has been written about images of God that might fit with or grow out of reflection on disability. To date, only three proposals stand out within the literature of disability and religion: the Accessible God, proposed by Jennie Weiss Block; the Interdependent God, proposed by Kathy Black; and the Disabled God, proposed by Nancy Eiesland.

The Accessible God

Jennie Weiss Block is a disability professional with an interest in theological metaphors for disability. She does not identify herself as a person with a disability but rather calls herself a "secondary consumer," a phrase commonly used to indicate a person who has a family member with a disability. In the book *Copious Hosting*, she proposes what she calls "a theology of access," the goal of which is to ensure "that people with disabilities take their rightful place within the Christian community."[23] This theology draws on principles from her experiences as a caregiver and advocate for people with disabilities and is specifically grounded in her belief that people with disabilities are a unique group not because they are in any way inferior to nondisabled people but rather because they are oppressed by society. She merges these principles with her own religious commitments, especially her belief that Christian communities have an obligation to challenge oppressive structures. Based on these ideas, she calls for church communities to make changes that lead to full access and inclusion for people with disabilities.

Block sees the lens of access and inclusion as a useful one through which to examine images of God. What does disability tell us about God? For Block, the answer is that disability is related to "the mystery of God's love and the great paradoxes of the Christian message."[24] In particular, from her Roman Catholic background, she writes, "Disability is a dramatic reminder that God's ways are not our ways."[25] While God cannot be fully known, she argues that the lens of disability highlights a God who is unfailingly committed to inclusion and access. She argues that "the mandate for access and inclusion is biblically based, central to our baptismal promise and commitment, and rooted in the Triune God."[26] This, she says, was the message of Jesus: all are welcome, and all have a place. According to Block, the New Testament account shows that Jesus included all people in his ministry, regardless of nationality, gender, background, or physical condition. For her, these stories of Jesus tell us what God is like, and what we are to be like as well. "Why a theology of access? Because the gospel of Jesus Christ is a gospel of access; creating access for those on the margins is a Christian mandate."[27]

Block's proposal is based on a social/minority group definition of disability, which highlights disability as an issue of oppressive structures and exclusion. Because of this, the Accessible God not only offers us images of inclusion but also calls for an end to oppressive structures. Block explains that this image

> demands we search our community with truth and face the serious reality that some of the people of God have been systematically denied access to the community . . . [and] demands that we admit that our own attitudes and actions have excluded people. It forces us to ask difficult questions. How can we become more inclusive? What actions do we need to take? What skills do we need? How must we change to make this gospel demand a reality in our communities? Becoming inclusive is a complex, demanding task that asks more of us than we are probably willing to give. It requires the traits of patience and vigilance that are in short supply in our fast-paced, outcome-oriented world. And yet, we cannot be faithful to our Christian vocation if we are not serious about the Christian mandate for inclusion.[28]

Based on her experiences as a disability professional and secondary consumer, Block argues that a theology of access demands the participation of people with disabilities in decisions that affect their lives. This is the emphasis of her work and the practical goal of her theological reflections. To highlight this point, she tells of a chapel that underwent extensive remodeling to become accessible to people with disabilities. In the process, however, the architects failed to consult anyone who actually uses a wheelchair. As a result, some arbitrary decisions were made that rendered the project inadequate to the needs of wheelchair users—the front door was not wide enough, the carpet was difficult to roll across, and not enough space was left for a wheelchair to turn into the "accessible" pew.[29] She uses this story to suggest that it is not only a practical error to exclude people with disabilities from decisions that concern them but also a theological error. Those involved in making decisions about the remodeling were not following the gospel mandate of inclusion and were not acting in a way that is consistent with the image of the Accessible God.

Thus Block is concerned not only with the image of God itself but also with the actions and responsibilities that such an image demands. Her theological reflection on the experiences of people with disabilities—and of those who care for and with them—leads her to a liberation theology that demands that God be on the side of justice, on the side of access. God favors accessibility over exclusion and thus calls for the church to be a site of access and justice. If we are to be like God, if we are to be in community with God, we too must join the struggle for access and inclusion with regard to all of God's people.

The Interdependent God

Kathy Black is a professor of homiletics who identifies herself as a person with a physical disability and who has worked for many years in Deaf ministry. Her interest is in the intersection of Deafness and homiletics, based on her experiences of "the Word made flesh" as a hearing person who preaches and teaches in sign language.[30] In *A Healing Homiletic*, she proposes what she calls a "theology of interdependence" that emphasizes her understanding of Christian community as a place where all are called to "work interdependently with God to achieve well-being for ourselves and others."[31] She begins with the idea that disability is a part of the everyday existence of millions of people and their loved ones. Her interest is in examining what significance this might have for theology if one rejects the notion that God causes disability. Her guiding question is "What can we as communities of faith believe that reconciles the reality of disability with our faith in a loving, compassionate God?"[32]

Black begins with the demand that we reexamine our images of God, specifically the notion that God is all-powerful. She rejects the idea of God as the great puppeteer, one who determines (or at least purposefully allows) both natural disasters and personal crises. She suggests that this conception would place God "in the position of being responsible for nuclear accidents, wars, rape, the hole in the ozone layer, homelessness, famine, toxic waste dumps, and earthquakes, as well as disability," consequences she finds unacceptable.[33] She argues that God is not a great puppeteer, but rather that human choice is one among many factors that determine our lives. Noting, for example, that causes for disability include genetic and environmental influence, she argues that "we are all interconnected and interdependent upon one another so that what we do affects the lives of others and the earth itself."[34] For Black, the stories of Jesus, especially the story of the resurrection, emphasize this connection. God is present in the midst of life and in the midst of suffering, offering possibilities for transformation. She argues that "the universe is interdependent, and God is a part of this interdependence."[35] Thus she takes phrases such as "the family of God," "communion of the saints," and "Body of Christ" to directly represent people who are interdependent with one another and with God, not only in times of crisis but also in daily life.

For Black, interdependence is a theological contribution that comes from the lens of disability. She suggests that most people with disabilities have an enhanced awareness that they are dependent upon someone or something, whether a sign language interpreter, a Seeing Eye dog, or a wheelchair. People with disabilities are conscious of such dependence, which in turn allows them to recognize that no one is totally independent. The experience of disability allows them to see what is sometimes invisible to others: all people, disabled or not, are dependent on other people and on the resources of the natural world for survival. She notes that this is a difficult awareness within the context of American culture, which values independence and sees dependence as something to be avoided. In the midst of this cultural context, Black sees Christian communities as one place "where people can be accepted for who they are as children of God, the place where dependency is acknowledged and interdependency is valued. . . . It is this interdependency in the midst of a culture that highly values independence that sets us apart."[36] Disability is a window into this insight. However, the Interdependent God is not only of or for people with disabilities, but rather is inclusive of and interdependent with all.

Black summarizes her position with this faith statement: "I do not believe that my disability or anyone else's is the will of God. I do, however, strongly believe that God's presence infuses our lives with strength and grace and love to manage whatever struggles come our way. God wills the well-being of each one of us at every moment of our lives."[37] Black notes that this well-being may be differently understood by each person, a lesson she has learned from Deaf Culture (where well-being is interpreted to include the condition of deafness). She also stresses that God is interdependent with us: "God depends on us to be God's agents of healing in the world as much as we depend on God to undergird us with everlasting love and care."[38] She relates the following story to explain:

> A little girl was late getting home from school. Her mother became more and more worried as the afternoon wore on. When she finally arrived, the mother said, "Where have you been? I've been worried sick!" The little girl responded, "Well, I was almost home, but then I saw Suzie sitting on the curb crying. Her dolly was broken." The mother, relieved, said, "Oh, so you stopped to help her fix her dolly?" The little girl with the wisdom of the universe said, "No. I sat down on the curb, and I helped Suzie cry."[39]

God is not the puppeteer, but instead "whenever we struggle in life, God sits beside us and helps us cry."[40] Perhaps when God struggles we are to cry as well. This image of God grows not from perspectives of privilege and power but rather from the lens of oppression and limitation. Yet this image, growing out of commitments to liberation, is not simply of or for the disabled. Black suggests that this image of the Interdependent God teaches all of us to be present with each other, acknowledging interconnection and valuing community, recognizing that we all depend on each other for life.

The Disabled God

The most powerful discussion of God to arise from within disability studies comes from Nancy Eiesland's proposal of the Disabled God, in the book by the same title.[41] Eiesland identifies herself as "a woman with disabilities, a sociologist of religion, and a professor at a seminary in the United States."[42] These three elements come together in her theology, which centers on what she calls "the mixed blessing of the body," especially related to the lived experience of disability. From her sociological perspective, she is especially interested in theories and methods that empower and provide a foundation for political action. She uses the image of the Disabled God to support such political action, particularly through processes of resymbolization. She is also interested in deconstructing notions of normalcy. She writes, "My own body composed as it is of metal and plastic, as well as bone and flesh, is my starting point for talking about 'bones and braces bodies' as a norm of embodiment."[43] Her proposal is a model of God that makes sense of her "normal" experience of embodiment, as well as one that supports and participates in the struggle for liberation of people with disabilities.

Eiesland argues that traditional images of God, especially those that lead to views of disability as either blessing or curse, are inadequate. Within the course of her own experience, she wondered whether such a God could even understand disability, let alone be meaningful to her. While working at a rehabilitation hospital, she asked the residents one day what they thought.

> After a long silence, a young African-American man said, "If God was in a sip-puff, maybe He would understand." I was overwhelmed by this image: God in a sip-puff wheelchair, the kind used by many quadriplegics that enables them to maneuver the chair by blowing and sucking on a straw-like device. Not an omnipotent, self-sufficient God, but neither a pitiable, suffering servant. This was an image of God as a survivor, as one of those whom society would label "not feasible," "unemployable," with "questionable quality of life."[44]

Eiesland made a connection between this image and the resurrection story in which Jesus appears to his followers and reveals his injured hands and feet (Luke 24: 36–39). She notes, "This wasn't exactly God in a sip-puff, but here was the resurrected Christ making good on the promise that God would be with us, embodied, as we are—disabled and divine. In this passage, I recognized a part of my hidden history as a Christian."[45] Eiesland suggests that Jesus reveals the Disabled God and shows that divinity (as well as humanity) is fully compatible with experiences of disability. The *imago Dei* includes pierced hands and feet and side. According to Eiesland, this Disabled God is part of the "hidden history" of Christianity, because seldom is the resurrected Christ recognized as a deity whose hands, feet, and side bear the marks of profound physical impairment. In the foreward to Eiesland's text, Rebecca Chopp notes, "The most astonishing fact is, of course, that Christians do not have an able-bodied God as their primal image. Rather, the Disabled God promising grace through a broken body is at the center of piety, prayer, practice, and mission."[46]

Like Block, Eiesland relies on the social/minority group model of disability, so that the relevance of the Disabled God is grounded in God's ability to be in solidarity with those who are oppressed. According to Eiesland, this image leads to "a deliberate recognition of the lived experiences of persons with disability, a critical analysis of a social theory of disability and of certain aspects of the church's institutional practices and Christian theology, and the proclamation of emancipatory transformation."[47] It is interesting to note that, unlike Black, who sees the Interdependent God as being for all people, Eiesland sees the Disabled God as being primarily for people with disabilities. She writes: "The truth of these theological statements is in their ability to transform reality, not necessarily for all people at all times, but for particular people in particular situations of oppression and pain. The truth of this liberatory theology of disability is in its ability to enable transformation for people with disabilities within the church and in its adaptability to addressing our ever-emerging challenges and opportunities."[48] For Eiesland, the image of the Disabled God makes it possible to bear an unconventional body. The image also opens the door to the theological task of rethinking Christian symbols, metaphors, rituals, and doctrines so as to make them accessible to people with disabilities. Eiesland's liberatory theology of disability comes from the perspective of people with disabilities and addresses people with disabilities as its central concern. She argues that this is essential not only for reasons of justice and inclusion but also because she believes that people with disabilities are most aware of their bodies and thus best suited to reflect theologically on issues of embodiment. She suggests that "the corporeal is for people with disabilities the most real . . . that is, we become keenly aware that our physical selves determine our perceptions of the social and physical world. These perceptions, like our bodies, are often nonconforming and disclose new categories and models of thinking and being."[49] For Eiesland, people who have experienced disability have an epistemological advantage: they see things that are invisible to others. As a result, any theology of disability must be done not only for, but also by, people with disabilities.

Based on her concerns with justice, Eiesland's image of God has specific characteristics. First, the Disabled God rejects the notion that disability is in any way a consequence of individual sin. She sees the scars of Jesus as verifying this claim: Jesus did not sin, yet he became disabled.[50] She argues that "injustice against persons with disabilities is surely sin; our bodies, however, are not artifacts of sin, original or otherwise."[51] The invitation to touch Jesus' hands and side also shows that taboos against disability are to be rejected, as well as that shallow expressions of sympathy and pity are inappropriate. The Disabled God provides an impetus for transformation and liberation in the lives of people with disabilities, just as the resurrection of Jesus provides an impetus for transformation and liberation in the world. The stories of the crucifixion and resurrection also lead Eiesland to reject the notion that God has absolute power; she argues instead that God is in solidarity with people with disabilities and others who are oppressed. This is a God who has experienced and understands pain and rejection. Eiesland suggests that the Disabled God emphasizes relationality over hierarchy, values embodiment in all its diversity, and provides a profound example of inclusion, love, and acceptance. As Eiesland summarizes: "A liberatory theology sustains our difficult but ordinary lives, empowers and collaborates with individuals and groups of people with disabilities who struggle for justice in concrete situations, creates new ways of resisting the theological symbols that exclude and devalue us, and reclaims our hidden history in the presence of God on earth."[52]

Building beyond these Models

The models presented by Block, Black, and Eiesland offer powerful alternatives to many traditional images of God. Each demonstrates that the idea of God is not incompatible with disability and, moreover, that God is for or on the side of people with disabilities. Each of the three models also claims that disability (as well as other human experiences) offers insight into God's nature. In the tradition of other liberation theologies, the three models presented here emphasize God's identification with people with disabilities, introducing both liberatory demands and claims about the intrinsic value of people with disabilities. The image of the Disabled God, in particular, has had a profound impact on many people with disabilities (e.g., almost every text or article on religion and disability published after Eiesland's book in 1994 includes a reference to the Disabled God). These are powerful metaphors, images that are meaningful and make sense for many people, and perspectives that highlight new possibilities for constructive theology. In addition, all three of these models deny notions that the religious practices of the able-bodied are the only relevant perspectives, and instead offer new opportunities for self-understanding and religious practice for and by people with disabilities. As Eiesland notes, "New religious images, values, and ideas about disability are essential as we seek to live our ordinary lives. Without them the barriers that people with disabilities encounter, while they may occasionally be lowered, will never be demolished."[53]

The models of the Accessible, Interdependent, and Disabled God offer novel and valuable perspectives on theology and disability. However, one must ask, do they go far enough? It is interesting to note that none of the three models described here are presented by theologians. Block is a disability professional, Black is a homiletician, and Eiesland is a sociologist. As Eiesland writes, "I did my graduate work in sociology but I'm a theologian by necessity."[54] Theologians have been largely absent from discussions of images of God that are relevant to the experience of disability. Unfortunately, that absence, as well as the simple fact that these discussions about disability and religion are still in their infancy, leads to a number of shortcomings. A central concern is that all three models lack sophistication about the nature and status of theological claims. These proposals stand outside the current debates about method and theological construction in which McFague, for example, has played a central role. Given that these three proposals are not meant to be complete theological proposals, my central interest is in the scope of the metaphors themselves, and this is where I will concentrate my analysis.

The image of the Accessible God, while powerful as an advocate on the side of those seeking inclusion and justice, is of questionable value once ramps are added and other barriers of architecture and attitude are removed. This is similar to many of the claims of the minority/social model of disability, where meaning is inherently tied to situations of oppression. Once such injustices are remedied, whether across the board or just in particular situations, the minority model has little remaining to say. While this may be relatively unproblematic for a political movement (or, at least, not worth worrying about until such a nondiscriminatory situation arises), it is less appropriate for a theological notion for at least three reasons. First, the image of the Accessible God only offers people with disabilities a sense that God is on their side. There is little in this image of God for them other than a sense of empathy or perhaps righteous indignation. It offers no clear direction in terms of action, devotion, or even imagination. Second, the image of the Accessible God lacks similar depth for religious communities and nondisabled individuals. This image demands justice and inclusion but proposes little else about God or about human life. It is a rather flat image, and as such it is hard to imagine how it might serve as a focal point for worship or community formation. Finally, as mentioned earlier, it is extremely unclear what value this image of God might have within the context of an inclusive situation. As such, not only is the image likely (hopefully) to become irrelevant or unnecessary, but it also offers little that would aid in the construction of an inclusive community aside from the demand that basic needs of access and inclusion be central. The image of the Accessible God is useful insofar as it criticizes inaccessible images and acts as a source of legitimacy or justification for access—which in and of itself is a worthy contribution—but the metaphor seems to offer little of value beyond that point.

Similarly, Black's notion of the Interdependent God has not yet been developed to a point at which it would be meaningful beyond its initial image. This model is reminiscent of McFague's work—namely, the recognition that all life is interrelated—but unlike McFague, Black offers little that would inform notions of person, ecclesiology, ethics, or eschatology. In part, this may be because Black does not develop her model in relation to any other theological issues but instead takes the Interdependent God as an illustration of the power of community and the importance of recognizing interdependence. It is possible that this image could be more fully developed—for example, she has recently begun to explore interrelationships between interdependence and ritual, including the creation of a ritual for the transition to use of a walker or an attendant.[55] However, this model allows little space for any of the messiness that often comes with real interdependence and community. Most important, Black's image does not address issues of power. To propose interdependence without including an analysis of power seems naive, and it weakens the foundation for her model. It is one thing to take the analogy of a Seeing Eye dog and propose from this that Christian communities should recognize and value their interdependence with each other and with God; it is another to look seriously at political, economic, and other relevant factors related to such interdependence. In this example, where is the interdependence for the Seeing Eye dog? What of the organization that trains the dogs, the donors who provide funding, the institutions that decide where the dogs will be assigned? Where is power located in this situation, and, according to the image of the Interdependent God, where ought it be located? Black's proposal also reminds us of feminist concerns about value placed on (inter)dependence without an adequate analysis of gender roles, another implication that an analysis of power would require. One must ask who among us needs to become interdependent, as well as whether this may serve as a fair and sufficient organizing principle for community or whether other values (such as trustworthiness or responsibility, for example) ought also to be raised. Black's image of the Interdependent God provides a useful illustration that counters traditional images of God, but it fails to address other significant issues related to community such as power and responsibility.

Eiesland's notion of the Disabled God, while an incredibly compelling image, also has significant limitations. One is that it leaves no room for individuals who might have an ambivalent or negative relationship with their own disability. Eiesland seems to assume that her audience accepts and embraces their experiences of disability as positive aspects of their identity. This draws significantly on the values of the minority model, which understands disability as an experience of oppression rather than a physical (or cognitive/emotional) situation. For individuals who define their disability in another way—for example, as a profound limitation of their life activities and choices, or as an experience of pain or suffering—Eiesland's model would be of little value other than perhaps suggesting that God may have empathy for their condition. Even then, a person who wishes to reject or overcome his or her own disability, or one who actively seeks healing from it, may find very little of value in a God who has a disability. Another area of concern that Eiesland fails to address is that the Disabled God is an anthropomorphic image, and thus carries with it the dangers (as well as benefits) found in many other such models. Eiesland suggests that her model is far superior to other person-centered images of God in that it embodies disability, but it is not clear that this image—any more so than other images of God—would be relevant to diverse experiences of disability. For example, one could question whether this model could be relevant to the Deaf community, to disability advocates, and to families of people with cognitive disabilities all at the same time. From Eiesland's model, we might be led to a plurality of Gods to represent the plurality of disability. It is also not clear, beyond the initial shock that God could be disabled or in a sip-puff wheelchair, what this God means or what relating to this God might necessitate. The picture itself is powerful, but we do not yet see what substance this image might hold beyond the initial revelation of God's situation of solidarity with disability as described by Eiesland and her discussion partners.

Each of the three models presented is limited in scope and audience, and is open to the same critiques applied to any other model of God. Even as the models highlight issues of concern in relation to disability, other issues are overlooked, such as racism, violence, and irresponsible consumption. The images only partially address the wide range of experiences of disability and fail to address how this diversity can be theologically represented. For example, could Eiesland's God be cognitively disabled?[56] Does Black's commitment to inclusion mean that separatists like some in Deaf Culture are not living in the image of God? Does Block's notion of the Accessible God have meaning for those who see disability as something other than as it is defined by the minority model? Each of these proposals presents us with a valuable perspective related to experience of disability, and each serves as a powerful corrective or complement to traditional notions that devalue or ignore experiences of disability altogether. It is easy to see how each of these can make a difference in the lives of people with disabilities and can be meaningful objects of reflection within religious communities. Yet each model is limited, both in terms of representing the wide variety of experiences of people with diverse disabilities and in its ability to be meaningful to temporarily able-bodied people of various identities, backgrounds, commitments, and concerns.

In some ways, this nascent literature proposing a liberation theology of disability is reminiscent of early movements and metaphors within other liberation theologies. Block, Black, and Eiesland demonstrate for us that there is a perspective from the underside, and new images of God, church, and other elements of theology that can come from listening to and engaging with people with disabilities and those who share their lives. As with other liberation theologies, they each propose a preferential option for the marginalized, imaging God in ways that show God's commitments to access, inclusion, and justice. They argue for the liberation of the oppressed and for the central role that theology must have in this process. As with other liberation theologies, these images and commitments can only be the beginning. We await a second generation of disability liberation theologians to add complexity and theoretical rigor to these already powerful images of inclusion and justice.[57]

To describe her struggle with images of God and the need for new images, Eiesland relates the following story:

> A man was wandering in a deep jungle not knowing where he was. Suddenly, he saw another man approaching him and so he called out, saying, "Help me, I'm lost." And the fellow who was approaching shook his head and said that he was lost too. But he did have one piece of advice. He gestured back over his shoulder and said, "Don't go that way, I've tried it already." Theologically, people with disabilities have tried most, if not all, of the well-trod theological paths in responding to our queries about the meaning of disability in the world. We have found them mostly treacherous and inaccessible.[58]

Eiesland argues that the existing theological paths are inaccessible, and that people who value the experiences of disability must forge our own paths. Drawing on the insights of the minority model, these early disability liberation theologians have given us images of what the new paths might look like and what commitments and possibilities they might include. We now have two possibilities for disability's contribution to theology: we can challenge existing theological models to include awareness of and attention to disability (chapter 3), and we can focus on liberative images drawing from experiences of oppression (chapter 4). In the next chapter, we will turn to the third way of imaging disability—seeing it as an expression of human limits—to explore the theological possibilities this image might offer.

5

Limits and
Disability Theology

Both the medical model and the minority model highlight aspects of
disability that are relevant for theological reflection: attention to the
diversity of human embodiment (i.e., there are disabled bodies) and
attention to justice concerns arising from observations of exclusion
and oppression (i.e., the lens of disability offers a unique and valuable perspective). This calls us to attend to embodiment and liberation theologies. Yet as was described in the first chapter, these two
perspectives are not our only alternatives as we reflect theologically
on experiences of disability. I have proposed that we also consider a
limits model, attending to the fluidity of human embodiment and
most particularly the claim that limits are an unsurprising aspect of
being human. Limits are normal. Rather than acting as a deficit, they
lead us toward creativity, and even toward God. In this chapter, we
will explore the possibilities of and implications for such a model in
constructive theology.

I begin with the claim that limits are a common and unsurprising aspect of being human. We may already know this, but it is also
something we tend to forget or reject. In common usage, the word
"limited" comes with a particular connotation, signifying a lack or
absence and emphasizing what cannot be done. It highlights barriers and constraints—one *is* limited. I propose an understanding of
limits that more positively connotes a quality of being. It emphasizes
a characteristic of humanity—one *has* limits. This proposal suggests
that limits, rather than being an array of unfortunate alternatives to

omnipotence, are an unsurprising characteristic of human nature. As Jeffrey Cohen and Gail Weiss note, "Simply put, limits need not foreclose. We are interested in what limits produce, . . . what they make possible, . . . what they incorporate, . . . as well as how the limits are themselves constructed in and through particular cultural matrices which they cannot escape but always exceed."[1] The term "limited" is often taken as representing something that is unfortunate and emphasizing that which is "not." The term "limits," on the other hand, places the emphasis on boundaries. When we reflect on human experiences of limits, we are reminded that boundaries, while often permeable, are also appropriate and necessary (as we see, for example, in psychological literature on differentiation and appropriate boundaries). Using the term "limits" highlights how each of us has these boundaries—none of us are omnipotent, for example—but does not carry the negative connotation that come with the alternative, "limited."

Approaching disability from the starting point of an assumed able-bodied "normality" leads one to think of "limited" and what is *not*. If we begin with a person who can walk and then look at one who uses a wheelchair, what is highlighted is what the person in the wheelchair *cannot* do. This has been our historically conditioned response to experiences of disability and is seen most clearly under the presuppositions of the medical model, where physical bodies are compared to a medical ideal and diagnosed in terms of what is lacking. However, an alternative perspective is suggested by the limits model. Approaching our understanding of humanity from the starting point of disability gives us a more applicable (or "normal," in terms of what is actually seen across the scope of the human population) vision of human limits. Limits may then be compared and considered, but they are not seen as abhorrent or abnormal.

The limits model proposes three significant religious claims that are not unfamiliar in the Christian tradition. First is the notion that limits are an *unsurprising* characteristic of humanity. This is a theme for many of the early Christian writers, who argue that humans are obviously and unsurprisingly different from God and also experience a dependence upon God. Other early writers suggest that humans are not perfect and static but rather experience processes of change and development, as can be seen in historical variations of language, culture, and understandings of the human body. From any of these perspectives, it is not surprising to note that humans have limits. A second and related claim suggests that limits are an *intrinsic* aspect of human existence—part of what it means to be human. This reminds us of the writings attributed to Paul which illustrate that each member of the community has a different gift and that it takes all of these differences together to create the body of Christ (1 Corinthians 12). Finally, the limits perspective implies that limits are *good* or, at the very least, not evil. Christians and Jews are reminded of their first creation story, where God saw all that had been created and said that it was good.

In contrast to these notions (but also represented by earlier authors), the familiar term "limited" leads us to a deficit model of anthropology. The focus is on what we lack. We lack certain abilities, and so emphasis begins to settle on one of three questions: Why do we experience these lacks (sin)? When will we overcome these lacks (heaven)? What is the alternative to the experience of limitation (God)? In contrast, the limits model presented here emphasizes the good (or, not evil) created nature of humanity. It explores how limits constitute our self-understandings and our relationality with others. It leads to an ethic of how we should act toward others. An example of the deficit model might be seen in Plato, who emphasizes the shadowiness of what we see and the absence of the real and true in the material world. The limits model, which might be termed a "gifts" model, can instead be seen in the writings attributed to Paul, who emphasizes how various gifts (as well as limitations) fit together to constitute a community.

The deficit model, highlighted by the term "limited," has served as the primary lens through which we see other anthropological claims. In liberation movements, we see challenges to specific claims of the deficit model, but even these still operate within the overarching lens of limited-ness. For example, we hear slogans proclaiming, "Gay is good" or "Women are strong." These claims, rather than challenging the deficit model as a whole, suggest instead that certain characteristics (gender and orientation) are not deficits as previously noted, but rather strengths or advantages (or are at least equal to their male or heterosexual counterparts). Disability theology could make similar claims, and in fact has done so within the social/minority group model. From this perspective, we hear that the real "handicap" comes from barriers of attitudes and architecture; the defect is not in the person with a disability but rather in the exclusionary structure of society. This logic does not challenge the deficit model but rather narrowly claims that disability itself is not a deficit—it changes which side of the equation we are on without actually challenging the equation. The attempt to normalize or contradict the specific analysis of the experience of disability as a deficit captures much of what has been said to date in disability theology.

This response is not adequate for disability theology. Unlike early examples from feminist or gay rights movements, disability is not a category that can be effectively revalued and reinterpreted through the process of comparison to its opposite. On the surface, this is a difficult challenge to grasp, because the disability rights movement has followed and imitated so closely the rhetoric and public policy initiatives of other liberation movements. However, disability is not a binary category. Disability varies from the popular conceptions of other movements in significant ways. To begin, if each of us lives long enough, we will become disabled. The same is not true of participants in other rights movements. In addition, disability is no one thing. At what point does my limp become more than a quirk and earn me the status of someone who is disabled? Even if we accept the relevance of the porous category "disabled," the individuals held therein often have much less in common, even in their physical functioning, than they do with individuals who are not identified as disabled. As was mentioned earlier, the limits model highlights the fact that a legally blind (disabled) individual may in some ways be more similar to a person who wears glasses (nondisabled) than to a person who uses a wheelchair (disabled). The signifier "disabled" attempts to hold a wide variety of bodily experiences, including mobility, sensory, and intellectual differences, in one designated category. As we have seen, this category is tenuous at best.

The limits model suggests that the insights that come from disability are something with which we all have experience. We learn the value of curb cuts when we use a stroller and the challenges of brick sidewalks when we use crutches for a sprained ankle. This model also highlights that limits go far beyond those labeled as part of the province of disability, and shows that some limits are viewed as more normal (I cannot fly) than others (I cannot run). The limits model challenges the deficit model, suggesting that disability is not something that exists solely as a negative experience of limitation but rather that it is an intrinsic, unsurprising, and valuable element of human limit-ness.

This chapter will explore the theological implications of the limits model for anthropology, reinterpreting limitation as part of what it means to be human rather than as a punishment for sin or an obstacle to be overcome in pursuit of perfection. In particular, this chapter will explore the nature of human diversity and suggest a reinterpretation both of traditional anthropological understandings and of images of God. It will also suggest that a limits perspective, rather than leading us toward fragmentation or universality, can instead offer a common ground for conversation and become a productive datum for theological reflection.

Interpreting Deafness

The experiences of the Deaf community were mentioned in chapter 1 as an especially interesting challenge to both the medical and minority models of disability. The signifier "Deaf" in this usage indicates the culturally Deaf—those who use sign language as their primary form of communication and who identify with the Deaf community—as opposed to the noncapitalized word "deaf" that indicates those who experience a loss of hearing. One can be deaf without being Deaf, and vice versa. Those who identify as Deaf often do not identify themselves as disabled, even though in most cases they are limited in their sensory ability to hear sounds. Instead, they consider themselves part of a linguistic minority. The arguments made by participants in Deaf Culture highlight the constructed and somewhat arbitrary (though still powerful) nature of the category of disabled. As was noted earlier, the concept "disabled" is inherently related to a society's concept of "normal." The category is a discursive construction, with shifting referents and shifting significance, a concept that demonstrates Derrida's notion of *différance*, the establishment of meaning through the assertion of difference.[2] When the Deaf argue that their identity comes from sharing a common language, they challenge any easy assertion of difference.

Deaf Culture's rejection of the category of disability is a way both of excluding themselves from a category that may or may not be relevant for others and of challenging the nature of such constructions altogether. Current Deaf alliances with "the disabled" are rarely based on identity but rather are strategic attempts to work for the achievement of rights for people by countering the essentialist view that people with disabilities are inherently pathological. The primary argument is that the Deaf are not an example of difference in the way we might assume—the difference comes from language, not from defect. Furthermore, as Davis observes, the Deaf "see their state of being as defined not medically but rather socially and politically."[3] If one equates disability with impairment, it would be a Hearing person who cannot sign who would be different and thus disabled within the context of a Deaf community.

While the "ableist" society sees individuals who cannot hear,[4] the Deaf instead see themselves as a distinct cultural group that uses a different language. This requires a change of perspective from those of us who are not Deaf. In contrast to the long history of writings that treat them as medical cases, or as people with disabilities who "compensate" for their deafness by using sign language, it is important instead to examine their world through an alternate lens, one that begins from their perspective and includes an examination of language, foundational myths, and communal identity. For the culturally Deaf, "their culture, language, and community constitute them as a totally adequate, self-enclosed, and self-defining subnationality within the larger structure of the audist state."[5] The term "audist" captures their perspective— it is a parallel to terms like "racist," "sexist," and "classist" and highlights how those who are not members of the Deaf community are biased toward the auditory mode of communication. The Deaf do not regard their absence of hearing as a disability any more than a Spanish-speaking person would regard his or her inability to speak English as an intrinsic disability (especially within the locus of a Spanish-speaking community). Rather, they see their group as a linguistic community, much the same as Hispanic or Korean subgroups in the United States.

Language is especially key to Deaf identity. The primary language spoken by the Deaf in the United States is American Sign Language (ASL). Common misconceptions of ASL suggest that it is either a collection of individual gestures or a code on the hands for spoken English. ASL is not based on the English language but rather has its own syntax, grammar structure, idioms, and vocabulary. It is a complete language in and of itself. It is a manual language in the sense that the hands play an important role as they make the signs, but the eyes, eyebrows, shoulders, mouth, head, and body stance are also contributing factors to the execution of ASL, conveying what we often think of as tone and inflection as well as grammatical markings. It has many complicated features that English does not have and is not considered an easy language to learn.

The signed gestures with which many in the Hearing community are familiar—whether through television or developmental services for preverbal children—are not ASL but rather Pidgin Signed English (PSE), which borrows vocabulary from ASL and grammar from English. With PSE a person can simultaneously use signed gestures and speak (or lip-sync) in English. In actual ASL, the rules for word formation include a complex verb morphology (including inflections for person, subject, and object) that does not resemble English. ASL also has an independent sentence structure. For example, in English it is correct to say either "I gave the book to him" or "I gave him the book," but in ASL only the second structure is possible, with the sign reading "I-give-him man book."[6] Signs often do not capture exact connotations for English words and vice versa. For example, the sign for "hearing" is commonly used to mean different from us (the Deaf). As a result, signing "a little hard of hearing" means a little different from us, and "very hard of hearing" means very different from us, even though an English translation would render "very hard of hearing" as closer in meaning to "deaf."[7]

A basic understanding of the elements of ASL is important because it reminds those of us who are not members of Deaf Culture that ASL is not simply an adaptation or translation of spoken English but a distinctive language with a unique structure. Language, however, is not the only difference between those who are culturally Hearing and those who are culturally Deaf.[8] Differences can be found based on the value given to speaking ability, use of eye contact, degree of body and facial expression, and concern with individual privacy. It is not uncommon for members of the Hearing culture to introduce themselves by name, but members of Deaf Culture typically introduce themselves by full name, school, and where they grew up. Conversational style often differs, with

Deaf conversations usually beginning quite informally, getting to the point quickly, and ending more slowly than one might find in a Hearing conversation. Deaf Culture also values deafness and greater degrees of hearing loss over hearing and lesser degrees of hearing loss, opposing the value scale within Hearing culture.

While American Sign Language is the common language for the majority of people within Deaf Culture in the United States, it has interesting geographic and racial differences (similar to accents and dialect in English), and it is not the same as the sign language used by Deaf persons in other countries. In Quebec, for example, Deaf French Canadians use Langue des Signes Québécoise. Nova Scotia has a community of Deaf people whose sign language is related to British Sign Language but not to ASL. Even within the population of Deaf people who use ASL, there is enormous diversity. Large communities of Deaf people in Boston, Chicago, and Los Angeles, to give a few examples, have their own distinctive identities. Within these larger communities there are smaller groups organized by class, profession, ethnicity, or race, each of which has yet another set of distinct characteristics. Members of Deaf Culture are often not only bilingual between signed and spoken languages but often necessarily fluent in a variety of signed languages as well.

Some members of Deaf Culture were born to Deaf parents and acquired signed language during early childhood. However, 90 percent of deaf children have Hearing parents and therefore are not assimilated into Deaf Culture from birth. Entrance into Deaf Culture for these children is often determined both by their parents' choice of communication methods and by their educational placement. Those who are educated in residential deaf schools will learn from other children as well as from Deaf adults who work at the school. In the informal dormitory environment children learn not only sign language but also the content of the culture. In this way, schools become hubs of the communities that surround them, preserving for the next generation the culture of earlier generations. Those who were educated in public schools may still become part of the Deaf Culture as adults, especially if they enter into significant relationships with other Deaf persons and become an active part of the Deaf community. Mainstreamed children may feel comfortable in both Hearing and Deaf worlds but may also be rejected by both—not totally accepted by the Hearing world but not as fluent in ASL and Deaf Culture (lacking the residential school experience) as if they were raised Deaf.

As with many other communities, Deaf Culture also has its own foundational stories. For example, according to popular legend, the origin of signed languages can be traced to the emergence of a large community that developed around the first public school for deaf children in France, founded around 1755 by Charles-Michel, Abbé de l'Epée, a French Roman Catholic abbot. The abbot was given the responsibility of teaching catechism to twin deaf girls so that they could take their first communion. According to legend, he became so enthralled with the concept of language and communication in inaudible modes that he eventually devoted his entire life to establishing the first school for deaf boys.[9] Great folktales have arisen about the abbot (ranging from extreme coincidences to supernatural powers), but at best he can be credited with having promoted the recognition of signed language—for all his efforts, he was not its inventor. The story of Epée (and similar stories about Gallaudet in the United States) has taken on great importance, however, as a foundational narrative about the creation of community.[10]

In addition to sharing a language, norms, history, and common foundational stories, the Deaf community is a community, at least in part, because it sees itself as one. This is perceived as a significant difference from the experience of other people with disabilities. Since most culturally Deaf people are reared in the Deaf community, go to the same residential schools, speak the same language, and participate in the same culture, they see themselves as radically different from other people with disabilities who, unless they take steps to become politically organized, are often isolated from others with their particular disability. As Davis notes, "Aside from self-help or social groups, people with disabilities have only relatively recently begun to think of themselves as a community. For example, if a person is born without a leg, or contracts polio or meningitis and loses the ability to walk or speak, that person is not automatically part of a culture, a language, a way of life."[11] Thus Deaf Culture "is not simply a camaraderie with others who have a similar physical condition, but is, like many other cultures in the traditional sense of the term, historically created and actively transmitted across generations."[12]

It is interesting to note that, as a cultural group, the Deaf have also been subject to cultural appropriation, especially in terms of their language. Kathy Black, a pastor and interpreter for Deaf religious communities, notes that almost any time she interprets to a mixed audience, Hearing people come up to her and comment on how inspiring the signing was, or how much more meaningful the worship was because of this added dimension. She notes that these Hearing people have minimal, if any, experience or knowledge of deafness and do not understand the language at all. For example, she tells this story from a graduation ceremony:

> I was interpreting and doing fine until the choir began singing in Latin. Thinking it was in English, I started signing what I thought I heard. Quickly I realized I had no idea what they were saying but

felt more awkward stopping after I had already started signing. There was no easy way off the stage so very gracefully I explained to the deaf people that I had made a mistake and that the song was really in Latin and what did they want me to do. They signed back from the pews that they wanted me to tell them a story, so I did. I told the story in perfect time to the music and ended, of course, when the choir ended. After the service, several hearing people came up to me and told me how inspired they were by the music interpreting. One woman had tears in her eyes and told me how she had experienced God in a way she never felt was possible. I did not have the nerve to tell her I was really signing a story about an elephant![13]

Perhaps the appropriation of Deaf Culture, whether it is the popular "I-love-you" sign or a more profound sense of feeling moved, is one of the clearest signals that the Deaf are not just a disabled group but rather a legitimate culture with all of the benefits and dangers therein.

An examination of Deaf Culture shows that to be deaf/Deaf is both a sensory and a cultural difference. In most cases, Deaf people are both Deaf and deaf, and their discussions and arguments over issues of identity show that these two categories are often interrelated in complex ways. Divisions are made along cultural and linguistic lines as well as on the degree of hearing loss. This is a challenging issue for members of the Hearing culture to understand. The interplay between sensory perception and cultural identity is an issue that has been the subject of little examination within the Deaf community, perhaps because many are so protective of their cultural identity that they choose to overlook the sensory implications. However, a close examination of Deaf Culture shows it to be more than just a linguistic minority group. As with other cultures, the specific characteristics of the community are at least in part connected to their situations of existence, including hearing loss, institutionalization, and experiences of difference. The cultural values named earlier in this chapter, for example, differentiate the Deaf from the Hearing based not just on ability to hear but on how one identifies oneself, how one begins and ends conversations, the extent to which gestures and eye contact are expected, and the value judgments placed on privacy and ability to hear. These concerns, while serving to define the Deaf as an independent cultural group, are not unrelated to sensory function and historical identity. Naming one's school, for example, both identifies how one came to join Deaf Culture and prepares the conversation partner for any regional differences in language. Beginning a conversation informally and getting to a point quickly is important when communicating without voice. Expectations for eye contact and gesture are unavoidable for almost any signed language. These cultural differences show it to be inaccurate to call the Deaf "just" a linguistic minority, as their identity is (at least historically) related to sensory function as well as community formation.

This point is important to the current project because it gives us an example of the importance of reflection on limits. There are good reasons why the Deaf often are uncomfortable with the label "disabled," especially insofar as they reject medical descriptions of their sensory and linguistic conditions. Yet at the same time, the conditions of their sensory limits are inseparable from Deaf identity as a whole. As was mentioned earlier, many people who are deaf (do not hear) do not identify with Deaf Culture. There are also some who identify as Deaf even though they are able to hear (particularly CODAs—Children of Deaf Adults—who are often raised in Deaf Culture and learn ASL as their primary language). As a whole, however, the existence of Deaf Culture is historically based on and continues to be related to the sensory experience of not being able to hear and of communicating primarily through signed language. The limits model offers one way to make sense of this configuration—that one's limits, while not interpreted as defects, can affect and support one's overall self and communal identity. Standing with the Deaf, I am comfortable rejecting the notion that the inability to hear is a negative characteristic, although many would argue this point. Yet it is unquestionably a limit. Deafness means there are things that one cannot do and does not have access to, whether these relate to pleasure (listening to music), convenience (ordering at a conventional drive-through window), or safety (hearing a standard fire alarm). There are adaptations to help one live comfortably within these limits. At the same time, we must also note that we tend to overlook many limits of Hearing people until we attend to the skills and enhanced awareness of a Deaf person, for example, that a Hearing person is typically not able to read lips or converse (as through ASL) across a large room. All told, the limits may not be negative, yet they are limits all the same.

A central argument of Deaf Culture goes something like this: Just because I am deaf does not mean that I am not as good (at whatever) as you are. It simply means I cannot hear. The limits model supports this notion—it simply means that we have limits. Yet "simply" is a deceptive descriptor in this case, because it allows us to dismiss too quickly an important factor. We all have limits, and it is important to not overlook this fact. These limits are important, and they contribute to self and communal identity, whether through the dramatic example of Deaf Culture, which rejects the label of disability altogether, or through other experiences of disability or limits. Some limits are viewed negatively, or are ones we seek to overcome. These interpretations are based on values and are deserving of reflection (ethical as well as theological). The limits model allows us to examine the values and choices involved in our attitudes toward limits, both specific and general. It also highlights the degree to which limits contribute to human identity, culture, and community.

The example of Deaf Culture is an especially interesting one because Deaf Culture contains clearly stated norms, values, history, and other cultural elements. This makes it an especially useful case to examine when looking at the interrelation of limits and identity. However, it is also important to look at other examples, ones that are perhaps more complicated. Let us now turn to a dramatically different example, one that is much more difficult to capture and one that has in fact been avoided by most work on disability studies: the case of cognitive disabilities.

A Different Difference: Cognitive Disabilities

An examination of the experiences of those with cognitive disabilities[14] shows some striking similarities to the experiences of the deaf/Deaf, including a long and troubled relationship with institutionalization. In fact, deaf and cognitively disabled individuals were frequently institutionalized together in the eighteenth and nineteenth centuries.[15] In addition, both deafness and cognitive disability have been analyzed as being constructed notions: they are conditions that do not exist in a vacuum but rather are defined by contrast to a conception of normal.[16] In his foundational work *Inventing the Feeble Mind,* James Trent notes that "mental retardation is a construction whose changing meaning is shaped both by individuals who initiate and administer policies, programs, and practices, and by the social context to which these individuals are responding."[17] Speaking of both deafness and cognitive disability, Davis notes, "These terms are all hopelessly embroiled in the politics of disability, or ability if you like."[18]

The example of cognitive disabilities also shows striking contrasts to Deaf Culture. One significant difference is that there is no "community" of the cognitively disabled. Unlike the case with the Deaf, who are often raised or schooled in the Deaf community, "if a person is mentally delayed, he or she cannot be said to be part of a culture of the mentally delayed."[19] Neither shared language nor cultural values can be named or distinguished from those of the nondisabled culture, and there is no foundational story, such as that of the abbé, to draw on for understandings of identity or community. There seems to be no broad culture or community of those who experience cognitive disability.

Cognitive disability is also an interesting case because it is an example of disability that does not even make sense under the auspices of the minority model. Questions of rights and of access often assume (and even rally around) claims that people with disabilities are just as able (often meaning "smart") as those without disabilities. Particularly within the academy, we have seen very little accessibility for or engagement with experiences of cognitive difference, and very little interest in it as a specific topic or category of concern.[20] Even in the wealth of recent works on disability studies, we see little mention of cognitive disabilities other than histories of institutionalization and sterilization. If mentioned at all, it is typically one addition to a list of various disabilities without any reference to specificity, just as disability itself is often seen as one addition to a list of various isms or particularities without any interest in specificity. It is our commonsense notion to refer to cognitive difference as "a disability," yet this has been the subject of little theoretical (or liberation-focused) work, and those who are cognitively different are often excluded from direct involvement in disability activism themselves. While few would question that those who are cognitively different are (at least in some ways) disabled, especially insofar as they experience oppression and exclusion as well as limits, models of disability have failed to engage or reflect upon cognitive disabilities in relation to disability studies as well as to human self-understanding in general.

Cognitive disabilities typically are categorized as substantial limitations in intellectual functioning. According to the American Association on Intellectual and Developmental Disabilities,[21] cognitive disability is "characterized by significant limitations both in intellectual functioning and in adaptive behavior as expressed in conceptual, social, and practical adaptive skills."[22] Cognitive disabilities are often labeled based on IQ test results (typically a score below 70), but they may also be identified on the basis of developmental delays observed during early childhood. People with cognitive disabilities may have higher than average functioning in some areas (such as art or memorization) but are, to varying degrees, identified as dependent on others for certain social and intellectual tasks. As with other disabilities, cognitive differences can be traced to a variety of causes, such as genetics (Down's syndrome), disease (rubella), or environment (fetal alcohol syndrome). It is important to note that, as with other instantiations of disability, the category here is not as solid as it might appear, and there is no "typical" cognitively disabled person.

An examination of the minimal literature on cognitive disability demonstrates an ongoing concern as to whether and how this category of people can be delineated. A wide variety of observations can lead to the label "cognitively disabled," including people who have impaired intellectual development, do not develop or learn as quickly as others, have a limited ability to learn and put learning to use, have a limited capacity in writing and arithmetic, or have difficulty acquiring social skills.[23] Some scholars argue "that the notion of the cognitively disabled is wholly culture relative and in fact a creation of the impact of modernity on Western societies."[24] They note that in preindustrialized communities, for example, one would find a much greater tolerance of intellectual variability. At other times, societies have banished the cognitively disabled or assigned them a status of less than full humanness. There have been many societal interpretations of cognitive disability, including defining it as a disorder of the senses, a moral flaw, a medical disease, a mental deficiency, a menace to the social fabric, or a variation in the cognitive continuum. Language reflects some of these attitudes: "outdated" words like "idiot," "imbecile," "feeble-minded," "moron," "defective," "and retarded," just as contemporary phrases such as "persons with mental retardation," "persons with developmental disabilities," "persons specially challenged," "or persons with special needs" all portray societal attitudes towards the category of cognitive disability.

While lacking a communal or foundational myth as with Deaf Culture, there is a long and important history associated with societal treatments of cognitive disability, including what are now interpreted as horrific stories of institutionalization, sterilization, and eugenics. A growing literature focusing on the mental hospital, but also relevant to cognitive disabilities, initiated a new era of study in the middle of the twentieth century. Erving Goffman's *Asylums* appeared in 1961.[25] Based on his personal observations, Goffman argues that mental hospitals operate as "total institutions." As such, hospitals strip patients of their individuality and separate them from people and systems that once supported them. Institutions enact physical and psychological control through the use of locked wards, common uniforms, lack of privacy, and institution-specific naming. Goffman identifies these controls as a form of mortification: the taking of life (as well as individuality) away from the patient. Patients often react to these conditions with hostility or other personality changes, thereby confirming the deviant label applied to them by the institution. Eventually institutionalized patients so thoroughly absorb the label of deviant (or sick, or crazy) that the control associated with total institutionalization becomes more a matter of routine than of necessity. According to Goffman, total institutions turn individual difference (in this case, of cognitive ability) into what we see as deviance and disease.

This principle was applied to cognitive disabilities in Wolf Wolfensberger's influential book *The Principle of Normalization in Human Services*.[26] Struck by Goffman's portrayal of the dehumanizing effects of the total institution, Wolfensberger began to construct a rationale for taking the responsibility of care away from the institution and, indeed, for changing the very vision of care. According to Wolfensberger, cognitively disabled people are seen as deviant because their "observed quality" is viewed "as negatively value-charged."[27] Wolfensberger argues that residential institutions, special school programs,

and sheltered workshops emphasize only the devalued qualities of the cognitively disabled, who then take on role expectations that reinforce the same
devalued qualities. Treated like children or as subhumans, people with cognitive disabilities assume these roles and act as expected. Wolfensberger and
others argue that, in order to change these role expectations, service providers
must work with the cognitively disabled to help them assume socially valued
behaviors and integrate them into culturally normative settings. Throughout
his work, Wolfensberger emphasizes a transition from notions of deviance
to demands for dignity—he claims that dignity cannot happen in (deviant-
producing) institutions but must be found in full participation in the mainstream of American life.

In recent years, Wolfensberger's model of normalization has become the
predominant framework for people with cognitive disabilities. The era of the
large state institution has passed, and more and more often people with cognitive disabilities live, work, and are educated in relation to the mainstream. As
Trent notes, "More capable retarded citizens hold full-time jobs, have families,
and pay taxes—and wreck cars, have extramarital affairs, and get audited by the
IRS."[28] Significant justice concerns remain, with few possibilities for meaningful job opportunities, a lack of funding for appropriate educational opportunities, and a high percentage of people with cognitive disabilities in prison and
on death row. Questions of identity linger as well. As Trevor Parmenter asks,
"Where do the people with an intellectual disability stand in society? Is their
position much changed from that of the previous two centuries? Have they
been emancipated from the phenomenon of 'otherness'? How can we articulate
a meaningful vision of community and social reality for this group?"[29] Even in
the contemporary move away from institutional power and control and toward
more creative notions of relationality and moral influence, people with cognitive disabilities are still identified as "other," are spoken to rather than spoken
with, and lack public opportunities for self-determination or claimed identity.

Nowhere is this "otherness" more apparent, and ironically so, than within
disability studies. As was discussed in chapter 1, the last twenty years have pro-
duced an impressive amount of scholarship regarding disabilities of all kinds as
well as a growing literature addressing the physical and theological accessibility
of Christian churches. However, the situation is quite different with respect to
cognitive disabilities. While some are attending to the inclusion of people with
cognitive differences or autism in worship or congregational life, these identities have not been addressed within disability politics or scholarship. Though
the point is seldom made explicit, intelligence is typically assumed to be central both to disability politics and to theological reflection and construction. As
Christopher Hinkle notes, "Many political and academic attempts to address

discrimination against those with disabilities reinforce, by their very nature, the equation of intelligence with human worth that marginalizes those who are mentally retarded."[30] It has become the norm for disability scholars to demand that liberation *for* people with disabilities come through actions taken *by* people with disabilities, as they uncover their own voice, worth, independence, and self-confidence—but cognitive disability does not fit neatly into this approach. As Hinkle notes, "The romantic idea that once all the barriers are removed and all the ramps are in place, we will all be equal participants in balanced conversation assumes equal intellectual abilities among the participants."[31] The liberation motif assumes that we are all equally capable, particularly in the area of intellect, and (to date) has made little attempt to address these assumptions. Disability rhetoric has not only been developed without the input of the cognitively disabled (who, for example, are seldom present at academic conferences), but disability movements also exclude both consideration of and presence of people with cognitive disabilities from the self-liberation that this rhetoric seems to demand.

Cognitive disability is difficult to theorize, perhaps much more messy and therefore less appealing than interpreting Deaf Culture. It seems not so much a project of cross-linguistic or cross-cultural dialogue as something quite different. At present, there are no narratives that express the experience of cognitive disability.[32] As Brett Webb-Mitchell notes, "The major problem is that first-person narratives of people with mental retardation have not been collected, heard, and understood by others. Without hearing their voice, we cannot understand their story."[33] Rather than hearing their stories, we imagine what they might be like, or study the developmental experiences of children (often cognitively nondisabled) rather than looking at cognitively different adults. Webb-Mitchell describes the situation in this way:

> People with mental retardation have been almost absent from our social gatherings, and the public has been kept uninformed of their condition in society. This problem of not being able to communicate with those who are disabled has a social history as those who are not-yet-disabled people have kept people with mental retardation hidden in institutions in rural settings, or brought them into group homes but rarely visited them or invited them to our congregation, or left them to wander the streets of our cities as homeless citizens.[34]

While some recent attention has been paid to community formation for people who experience cognitive difference (specifically through the L'Arche movement) and to the inclusion of those with cognitive disabilities into religious worship experiences, little attention has been paid to cognitive disability as a category with theoretical relevance for disability studies.[35]

While disability scholars argue that our disciplinary commitment "means not distinguishing between 'good' and 'bad' disabilities, refusing to stigmatize people with intellectual disabilities as inherently more impaired than those with ambulatory disabilities, for example,"[36] cognitive disability is still marginalized. It is an issue that is foreign (we do not see people with cognitive disabilities in the academy), threatening (it raises significant ethical and philosophical questions about the nature and characteristics of humanity), and even frightening (especially for those of us who love our intellectual abilities). Within a discourse dominated by intellectual and academic rigor, it is hard to know where an entry point for the cognitively disabled may appear. Yet insofar as we believe that people with cognitive disabilities are people, or even, with McFague, as we see them as part of the body of God, the experience of cognitive disability is unavoidable as we consider and theorize what it means to be human.

Limits and Theological Anthropology

The preceding discussions of Deaf Culture and cognitive disabilities highlight some of the messiness that comes from reflection on actual embodiment. Even in the attempt to explore and emphasize difference, this discussion itself is also an exercise in categorization (i.e., it would have been a different project to look at actual Deaf and cognitively disabled individuals) and in distance (speaking of others rather than of myself). The argument made earlier that McFague did not attend adequately to the full diversity of human life is one that could be offered against this project as well. However, even glancing from a distance at these two broad examples of embodied particularity offers theological insights that "enflesh" the limits model, while simultaneously offering depth to our earlier analysis of McFague's model of the body of God.

McFague grounds her notion of anthropology in discussions of space and place. These two categories are helpful for making sense of identity issues for the Deaf and cognitively disabled. For the Deaf community, a key concern has been with finding their place—not as unequal participants in the Hearing world, but in their own communal home, with their own values and norms. Insofar as the Hearing community has denied the Deaf their space, or has made our space inaccessible to visitors from this other "land" (e.g., failing to install TTYs or to arrange for interpreters at academic conferences), we are guilty of McFague's sin of "Us versus Us." For those with cognitive disabilities, the issue of space and place is relevant as well. The era of institutionalization attempted to keep "them" out of "our" space and to limit the (financial and other) resources that were given to their space. McFague would identify this as a lie that fails to acknowledge our shared history (from the common creation story) and our shared home (the earth or the body of God which we all inhabit). Space and place, for McFague, also include a sense of responsibility for the other—we must not abuse the resources (and habitat) of others, and we must recognize that "we" have a special responsibility as the ones who are self-consciously self-conscious.[37] Attempts at normalizating (or mainstreaming) the cognitively disabled could be understood as being successful only insofar as we share all of our space (not just allowing them to bag our groceries but creating real opportunities for employment, socialization, and recreation) and are respectful of their needs, broadly defined by McFague to include "loving families, education, medicine, meaningful work, . . . music, art, and poetry"[38] or whatever else might be most appropriate. Rather than sinful selfishness, we must acknowledge our home (the earth) to be their place as well as ours.

The notion of limits offers an additional facet to this example. In the limits model, the fact that all people are limited to varying degrees is highlighted. The binary categories of "us" and "them" are challenged. We recognize that it is not only those who are labeled "disabled" that experience limits; limits are something inherent in the experience of humanity. Rather than identifying this as an inherently negative or evil characteristic, limits are understood to be part of creation. This does not mean that we ought not strive to overcome or adapt to limits; rather, it highlights that our interpretation of limits is based on values that are appropriate for ethical and theological reflection, and that alternate interpretations are both possible and appropriate. Under this model, Deafness may be valued as a difference rather than interpreted simply as a defect, and cognitive disabilities may be considered an appropriate subject for theoretical and theological reflection rather than simply categorized as an abnormality. However, the limits model does not stipulate that all limits are necessarily "normal" or even "good." It is much more complicated than this. The debate over cochlear implants raises very significant questions as to whether one would (or should) choose to be Hearing rather than Deaf. The example of cognitive disabilities, including the ways in which it is difficult to interpret and theorize, also attends to the notion that embracing all limits as "normal" or desirable is a very difficult thing even to imagine. Limits are, by their nature, limiting. Much of human history shows a creative demand to overcome limits, whether it be in the form of traveling faster, communicating over longer distances, or extending life. It is not the argument of the limits model that we should all want to be disabled, or even that we should embrace and be happy about all our limits. The importance of this model is its demand that limits, as well as the diversity of ability, must be seen as integral elements of our understandings of self and other, as key characteristics for reflection in a theological anthropology.

The implications of limits for theological anthropology are not confined to understandings of disability. One interesting example of the applications of a limits model (though not identified as such) can be seen in the ethical work of Sharon Welch.[39] Welch describes her anthropology as postmodern humanism, a phrase that she notes is itself a contradiction in terms. She defines this as

> a turn to humanism as the site of engaging different claims about not only social policy but also the very nature of good and evil, of justice, order, power, and chaos. Feminists, men and women involved in the Religious Right, in communitarianism, in the politics of meaning, all are engaged in the construction of group and individual identity, in often mutually exclusive constructions of what it means to be human. To turn to humanism, then, is not to find an answer, an ahistorical or essential resolution to this debate, but rather to name what is at stake—radically different constructions of order, radically different ways of engaging chaos, radically different views of what sustains creativity and community, of that which prevents injustice and cruelty.[40]

For Welch, key to this project is an acknowledgment of limits. As she writes, "To acknowledge one's limits includes acknowledging the limits of others, and it also includes acknowledging the potential wisdom and insights of others as well as of oneself."[41] Similar to my own argument, Welch suggests that the existence of limits is not necessarily negative but rather is an unavoidable part of being human. This perspective on limits leads to her ethical proposal:

> From this matrix of seeing ourselves as flawed—but without attributing to that flaw fall, shame, or guilt—there can emerge a nondualistic vocabulary of strength and weakness, of insight and deception—one that emphasizes accountability, not guilt, a sensibility that encompasses a good-humored recognition of the accidents, the surprises, the muddles that characterize our attempts to implement the good.[42]

Welch argues that, if we recognize our limits, the American dream and American despair are no longer our only options. By embracing limits, we are instead able to construct and embrace a national identity that includes success and failure, prosperity and loss, freedom and restriction. This nondualistic vocabulary and acceptance of limits allows us "to create and resist without the illusion of progress . . . to live fully and well without hopes for ultimate victory and certain vindication."[43] Acknowledgment of limits means neither defining ourselves in terms of perfection and thinking too highly of ourselves as individuals or as a community/nation (uncritically accepting or expecting the American dream) nor defining ourselves based on what we lack and thinking too lowly of ourselves and our community/nation (falling into despair, cynicism, or apathy). Instead, it offers us an ethic that makes sense of who we are and what we want to be, without depending on illusory goals that fail to acknowledge the realities of human individual and communal existence.

The limits model demands that we reject unrealistic ideals or illusions of perfection, recognizing that such images lead to unproductive and dangerous dualisms, such as the ones examined by Welch. The limits model suggests instead that we recognize that limits are a normal and unsurprising aspect of humanity, a recognition that leads us to new ethical and relational formulations. This perspective provides an essential starting point from which we may begin conversations and reflections on undertheorized facets of human embodied experience, including Deafness and cognitive difference. It calls for a reexamination of dualistic categories such as disability, recognizing that these are sometimes arbitrary constructions that, while having some political importance, also act to divide and oppress. At the same time, the suffering that does occur related to disability or limits should not be diminished. This perspective allows us to reflect on our interpretations of limits as well as to identify areas where our limits become disabling due to social or physical barriers. Rather than leading us to fragmentation or universality, the limits model offers a ground for conversation and a standpoint from which to challenge exclusionary constructions of difference.

The preceding discussion has proposed that the limits model provides a helpful way to approach anthropological considerations. It offers a useful framework for understanding issues of community (including Deaf Culture and notions of America), as well as what we might sometimes define as individual constitution (what is cognitive disability, how do we make sense of disability in general). These are valuable questions and ones that are difficult for us to recognize when we fail to attend to the limits experienced through disability. Yet if we are exploring the possibilities of this model for constructive theology, we must also attend to its implications for our understandings and interpretations of God.

Limits and God

Reflection on bodies leads us to an awareness of limits, which clearly has significant anthropological implications. The notion of limits has potential for descriptions or understandings of God as well. If, as McFague claims, the body of God includes all bodies, or if, as we read in Genesis 1, humans are created in the image of God, we must then ask what it tells us about God that humans are limited. This question can be fruitful within both the medical model (is God's power limited?) and the minority group model (does God understand oppression and exclusion?). The limits model brings in a new perspective that asks questions about the nature of God's creation as well as the nature of God's being. McFague highlights the process of naming, which she argues is just as important as action; as she writes, "What we call something, how we name it, is to a great extent what it is to us."[44] The limits model highlights that our limits are an unsurprising part of being human, and at the same time identifies areas where limits become disabling due to social or physical barriers. Similarly, this idea of limits is also relevant for our understandings of God. When we think of limits, we think of limit-ed. We tend to imagine that a God with limits (e.g., a God with an impairment) is less (at best) or defective (at worst). Why would we worship, or even want, a limit-ed God? If God has an impairment, we tend (from a limited-ness perspective) to think of what God is *not* (a blind God cannot see, a deaf God cannot hear). However, applying the limits model may instead give us a very different way to think of God.

When we imagine an unlimited God, there is a subtle implication that the more limits we have, the less we are like God. This is reminiscent of Daly's claim that if God is male, then the male is God. If God is unlimited, then the less limited are more like God, and the more limited are less like God. The notion that God includes limits counters this implication. This is relevant not only for people with disabilities but also for all of us who experience limits to varying degrees. To use McFague's criteria, a metaphorical understanding of God that is open to limits is consistent with both the Christian tradition and contemporary science. Even some of the most traditional, anthropomorphic notions of God suggest that God took limits willingly—for example, by creating or allowing free will, or by taking on personhood (and death) through Jesus. Both contemporary science and postmodernism include claims about limits: finite resources, partiality of knowledge, and fluid borders and boundaries. A notion of God that includes limits is consonant with these contemporary understandings of finitude, and even with experiences of decay and death.

Imaging God as including limits has a number of positive benefits. The notion of limits as applied to God teaches us, for example, that "disability does not mean incomplete and that difference is not dangerous."[45] Such attention to limits can add to our understandings of God. For example, reflecting on experiences of disability, limits might be seen to speak to at least three characteristics: perseverance, strength, and creativity. People with disabilities often have to work harder than the able-bodied to gain access to buildings, education, decent wages, or relationships. Such characteristics of perseverance that come when one seeks to live with limits might also be characteristics that we would find in or wish to attribute to God. Limits also speak to strength, as people with disabilities are often stronger in at least some ways than "normals" (as anyone who has used crutches can attest). Such strength is often one of the attributes given to the divine. The existence of limits also speaks to creativity, as we all (whatever our limits) develop alternatives and work to compensate for what we cannot do, whether designing a new wheelchair or developing a satellite. The human proclivity toward creatively adapting to our limits might be a character-istic represented in a limits God. Limits might show a God that values creativ-ity, and the variety of limitations might show a divine preference for diversity. Finally, recognition of the sin of Me versus Myself that I proposed in chapter 3 might highlight an image of God as one who neither exaggerates nor denies limitation and instead is represented as an authentic and fully grounded self.

My proposal here is that, when we think about God, it is important to rec-ognize the existence and "normalcy" of limits. Limits do not tell us all that God is or all that we are, individually or as communities. As McFague would argue, it is at best one piece of the puzzle, one square of the quilt. Or, more modestly, it is one question to ask, one lens to try on: How do our understandings of self and God make sense of the fact that we all experience limits, that some limits are seen as more natural than others, and that limits are much more ambigu-ous than we often think? Rather than thinking of limits solely in a negative sense (what we, or what God, cannot do), this perspective offers alternatives for thinking about boundaries and possibilities. In an age of war, terrorism, economic injustice, and environmental risk, a recognition and theological af-firmation of limits seems more responsible than apathy or omnipotent control and offers a perspective that can lead to hopeful possibilities of perseverance, strength, creativity, and honest engagement with the self and the other.

The liberation models presented by Block, Black, and Eiesland demon-strate some of the insights that can be gained from a reflection on experiences of limits, particularly the experience(s) of disability. McFague's metaphorical approach makes a significant contribution to these models, suggesting that multiple metaphors are needed and that each metaphor must be open to evalu-ation and critique. In addition, McFague's model of the world as the body of God presents us with an even more basic metaphor from which to enter our re-flections on the image of God from the standpoint of embodiment. Just as both the medical model and the minority model of disability offer a significant lens but not a complete picture, the theological proposals offered by body-attentive theologies and by disability liberation theologies offer important pieces but do not capture the entirety of theological possibility. My proposal that we explore the perspective of limits offers additional possibilities for theological reflection and constructive images of God, especially insofar as it complicates our notions of able/disabled, encourages us to think of limits as a relevant aspect of human embodied experience, and invites reflection on attitudes and practices in relation to various limits. Critical reflection on embodiment has the potential to keep us grounded—embodied, as it were—in an understanding of limits and both what they enable and what they make difficult. This is the perspective offered by the limits model, one that I think is essential for theology, both as we contribute our reflections to issues of justice and issues of individual and communal identity and also as we propose images of God that represent and reflect these diverse embodied experiences.

Conclusion

Embodied Limits and Constructive Possibilities

The thesis of this work has been that critical reflection on disability has the potential to clarify and expand theological models, offering a significant contribution to the fields of both theology and disability studies. We have seen that it is valuable for contemporary theologians and religious thinkers to consider and reflect upon bodies in diverse manifestations of embodiment, and that existing theological models can be challenged to include awareness of and attention to disability. This draws on the most simplistic proposal of the medical model—that there are bodies that exhibit variations of ability and difference—but rejects the medical model's value claim that these bodies are less important than so-called normal bodies or that they are in need of repair. We have also seen the beginning of a literature that might be described as a disability liberation theology. This approach builds on the minority model's observation that people with disabilities face significant discrimination and oppression in society, and focuses its theological claims on concrete issues of liberation and justice.

While the medical and minority models are, at present, the two most common ways of understanding disability, we have noted that these models fail to capture the full diversity of experiences of disability—which may exhibit fluidity over time and situation—and also make little sense of experiences such as chronic pain. In response to calls for a third way, I have proposed attention to limits as a complement to the existing models. This new model attends to human diversity by recognizing the prevalence of limits and by rejecting dualistic categories and negative valuations. The limits model highlights the fact that human limits need not (and perhaps ought not) be seen as negative or as something that is not or that cannot be done, and instead claims that limits are an important part of being human—a fact that is overlooked when we reflect on the human body as generic. The limits model also reminds us that "normal" bodies are not as much the norm as we might think, and that it thus is inappropriate for an ideal or imaginary normative body to be the starting point for our theoretical or theological reflections.

The limits model offers a way to add necessary complexity to our theological and anthropological reflections. This complexity should come as no surprise: we know that bodies are leaky, messy things, and both philosophy and theology have repeatedly struggled with what it means to have limits—including the ultimate limit, death. The presence of limits is, in fact, more "normal" than their absence. This leads us to the theological claim that the recognition of limits ought not be tied uncritically to interpretations of value and worth. We are also aware that experiences and interpretations of limits change across time, as some limiting conditions are eliminated (polio) and others arise (carpal tunnel and chronic fatigue syndromes). The claim of the limits model is not that we should refuse to overcome or adapt to limits, nor that we should give up on medical advances or adaptive technology. It is still appropriate to suggest that some limits are to be rejected, including those that cause harm to self and others (alcoholism, violence, poverty). We need McFague's notion of space and place, or other criteria for evaluation, to help us understand which limits are "good" and which are "wrong," which to embrace and which to creatively overcome. The limits model provides a first step in this process of evaluation, allowing us to see assumptions and barriers, helping us to move beyond labels toward a more fully grounded view of embodiment.

It is my argument that disability and other experiences of human limits are interesting and worthy of religious and theological reflection. This also has significance for disability studies. While progress has been made in recent years toward disability rights as well as toward the advancement of the field of disability studies, we are becoming aware that current interpretations of disability, as delineated by the functional/medical and social/minority models, are not sufficient for reflection on experiences of disability and diverse embodiment. As with any model, each perspective highlights certain facets and overlooks others. One might consider the experiences of two wheelchair users: one paralyzed from birth, another paralyzed in a skiing accident. Neither the medical nor the minority model differentiates between these two experiences. The medical model sees similar physiological conditions: an inability to walk and a loss of sensation and motor skills in the legs. The minority model would see similar experiences: barriers of architecture and attitude due to societal interpretations of wheelchair use. The limits model offers a third way, a new perspective, one that allows us to reflect on each individual's unique experiences, recognizing that what is interpreted as normal or limiting by each individual may be quite different. The limits model recognizes that these two individuals may vary in terms of their attitudes toward their disabilities, their own definitions and understandings of disability, and the way and degree to which they see limits as affecting their lives. Additionally, neither the medical nor the minority model attends appropriately to the fluidity of disability as a category, especially insofar as all people experience limits to at least some degree. Because the limits model begins with reflection on distinct experiences of embodiment, rather than with assumptions of normalcy or political convictions, it allows for a diversity of interpretations and meaning-making. Both the medical and the minority models are valuable for the perspectives they offer, but even together they do not fully capture the complexity of experiences of diversity or human embodiment. The limits model adds a necessary component that is lacking in other models.

Recognizing that knowledge also has limits, the proposal of the limits model necessitates conversation, interaction, and relationship. Both theology and disability studies can benefit from such conversations. Theological efforts, including the recent "body craze," need to attend to the full diversity of experiences of human embodiment in order to be authentic and appropriately grounded. Disability studies can contribute not only an awareness of the existence of disability but also a sense of the complexity of varied instantiations of disability. From the other side, disability studies needs a conversation partner and a place where its own normative claims can be examined and challenged. Theology can contribute its own critical interest in reflecting upon what it means to be human. Conversations between disability and theology can be mutually beneficial, allowing us to challenge problematic metaphors and oppressive practices as well as to imagine new possibilities for theoretical and theological contributions.

We must consider the implications of diverse human experiences of embodiment in our theological reflections and religious practices. Rather than proposing a single theology or a single image of God, this is a project with an uncertain and indeterminate end. It expands McFague's model by demanding reflection on actual experiences of messy, complicated embodiment, including the prevalence of limits. It challenges disability studies to engage with theology to explore constructive responses to such experiences of limits. This model invites each of us to move beyond sinful deception into fuller embodiments of care and community by being more open to our own individual limits and abilities. By encouraging us to look more closely at ourselves and each other, the limits model offers significant possibilities for theological reflection, interpretation of disability, self-understanding, and communal practice.

The perspective of the limits model cannot tell us all that God is, or all that the church should be, or all that we are as individuals or as communities, but it does tell us something vitally important. As McFague might note, it is one piece of the puzzle, one square of the quilt, but one that is both illuminating and essential. Reflection on disability should not scare us, and it should not be taken as theologically uninteresting. The limits model does not aim to dismiss or deny experiences of evil or suffering, nor does it devalue efforts to overcome limits—it does not propose that all limits are good or that we ought to embrace or accept them all. Rather, this model recognizes a complexity of experiences and offers a possibility for interpretation and sense-making. It allows us to recognize and reject some of our "blind" spots, including overwhelming biases against certain limits, and also allows us to evaluate and struggle with limits that are problematic or unjust. Challenging these conventions makes us think in new and unfamiliar ways not just about embodiment but also about anthropological assumptions and ideas about the nature of God. The limits model also allows us to imagine new possibilities, focusing on characteristics such as perseverance, strength, and creativity. Critical reflection on embodiment has the potential to keep us grounded, embodied as it were, in understandings of what certain limits may enable as well as what they may make difficult.

Rather than interpreting disability as something that is theologically uninteresting or that belongs solely to the realm of care, we have seen that disability can make a valuable contribution to theological reflection. Existing models need to be evaluated based on how well they can attend to experiences of disability, and space needs to be made for new liberation theologies of disability. Beyond this, we also need to be more intentional in our consideration of human limits, not just as they exhibit themselves in situations of disability but as we all experience them throughout our lives. When we are willing to acknowledge that limits are a normal and unsurprising aspect of human life, a whole new world of theological reflection opens to us. The limits model suggests that we must challenge existing dichotomies of us and them, recognizing instead a fluidity of limits. It suggests a new lens for the understanding of self and of community in a postmodern age and invites conversation with other discourses of embodiment and difference. The model can open us to new perspectives on characteristics such as creativity and ingenuity, attending to the benefits that can come from engagement with limits. It also offers us new ways to attend to our environment—including which limits are accommodated and which are not—and has significant implications for the analysis of power and responsibility. In these ways and many others, the perspectives that come from engagement with disability and embodied limits are essential for theology, contributing theoretical complexity to real issues of justice while simultaneously offering possibilities for new images and theological constructions that attend appropriately to human embodiment and diversity.

My local university campus posts a banner over the student center each September that reads, "Know no limits." The proposal of this book is completely the opposite: know all limits. Limits are a normal and unsurprising aspect of life. Yet we choose, for whatever reason, to stigmatize some and normalize others. When we dismiss disability as being an exceptional and othering experience, we deny the normality of limits in all of our lives, pretend that we do not experience increasing limits as we age, and even refuse to acknowledge the future limit of death. In these denials, we live a lie, a lie that harms other people (those on whom we project and reject these limits), the environment (when we pretend that it also has no limits), and even our selves. We can no longer consider what it is to be embodied—to have race, gender, sexual orientation, power, politics, religion—without also considering what it is to have embodied limits. We can no longer ignore reflection on experiences of disability and other embodied limits in our theological constructions. We must attend to the values that we place on limits, including on people with visible and profound limits, and must challenge our notions of what it is to be normal.

This book proposes some first steps in such a process. Yet the work has only just begun. What does it mean to construct theology from a perspective that values human limits, one that embraces experiences of disability as normal? How do we make sense of our desires for health, long life, and the absence of pain within such a perspective? How might a theology of limits interact with other justice concerns that focus on social construction or that may perhaps reject "limits" as an appropriate description of embodied difference? The challenge of this book—to examine and embrace and reinterpret our limits—is by no means an easy or uncomplicated proposal. Because of our individual limits, this is also necessarily a communal project. As we explore together our limits and the things that these limits make possible, we are called into new visions of ourselves and of each other in a beautifully diverse world. We are called into limit-ness, to being fully present in our embodied limits. This opens us to a theology of possibility, of becoming rather than being, of movement rather than stagnation. The recognition of limits opens us to new understandings of creativity, community, and interdependence. It allows us to share the stories of our wishes and our fears and to reflect theologically and ethically on these experiences and values. It opens us to life as we actually live it. It comes out of reflection on the complexity of disability, and it deliberately embraces experiences of disability, but it does not stop there. In the ways I have suggested in these pages, and in others not yet even imagined, a theology of limits has great potential to benefit us all.

Notes

INTRODUCTION

1. Bureau of the Census, *Press Release CB06-FF.10–2* (July 2006).

2. Bureau of the Census, *Census 2000 Special Report 23: Disability and American Families* (July 2005).

3. Bureau of the Census, *Press Release CB06-FF.10–2* (July 2006).

4. World Health Assembly, *Document A58/17: Disability, Including Prevention, Management, and Rehabilitation* (April 15, 2005).

5. Longhurst, *Bodies,* i.

6. See, for example, Gallop, *Thinking through the Body;* Hancock, *The Body, Culture, and Society;* Camporesi, *The Incorruptible Flesh;* Longhurst, *Bodies;* Gallagher and Laqueur, *Making of the Modern Body;* Shildrick, *Leaky Bodies and Boundaries;* Tambornino, *The Corporeal Turn;* Brook, *Feminist Perspectives on the Body;* and Davis, *Embodied Practices.*

7. Hannaford and Jobling, *Theology and the Body;* Raphael, *Thealogy and Embodiment;* Law, *Religious Reflections on the Human Body;* Bekkenkamp and de Haardt, *Begin with the Body;* Coakley, *Religion and the Body;* Ellison and Thorson-Smith, *Body and Soul;* Isherwood, *Good News of the Body.*

8. In the sections that follow, I will typically refrain from putting "normal" or "healthy" in quotation marks, but I hope that readers will recall that such terms should be regarded with suspicion. As later sections of this work will show, the model I propose challenges the notion that any one of us is, or can be, normal, as well as the notion that anyone can describe what a normal body is.

9. Audience members voiced a competing concern that the discipline of disability studies not become ghettoized or marginalized by limiting entrance to those with recognizable impairments. Similarly, competing tensions

related to insider/outsider designation can be seen in other identity issues, such as race, gender, culture, and religion.

10. An interesting exception, to which I will return later in this book, is that the field of disability studies often shows a prejudice against those with cognitive or emotional disabilities.

11. Titchkosky, *Disability, Self, and Society*, 10.

12. See Foucault, *Madness and Civilization*.

13. And, as I will argue later in this work, they rarely fit for most others as well.

14. Anderson, *Graduate Theological Education and the Human Experience of Disability*, 57.

15. I have elsewhere described this as a "limit-ness" model to further accentuate the distinctions between this proposal and the negatively valued connotation of the more common word "limitedness." See Creamer, "The Withered Hand of God," and Creamer, " 'God Doesn't Treat His Children That Way.' "

16. Davis, *Enforcing Normalcy*, 1.

17. Davis, *Bending Over Backwards*, 25.

18. Ibid., 10.

19. Davis, *Enforcing Normalcy*, 2.

20. Ibid., xvii.

21. Because of the diversity of experiences held within the one category "disability," I would argue that this partiality is the case for all who do disability studies—a person in a wheelchair cannot fully know the experience of someone who uses American Sign Language as their primary mode of communication.

22. Rosemary Radford Ruether has recently critiqued this view that "early feminism" was exclusive and universalizing as overly simplistic. See Ruether, "A White Feminist Response to Black and Womanist Theologies."

23. bell hooks, *Feminist Theory*, x.

24. Ibid., 18.

25. Welch, "Sporting Power," 174.

26. Ibid., 183.

27. A term used by hooks and others to highlight a lack of attention to women of color.

28. hooks, *Feminist Theory*, 15.

29. Briggs, "The Politics of Identity and the Politics of Interpretation," 173.

30. Bartky, "Foreword," in *Men Doing Feminism*, xii. See also Jardine and Smith, *Men in Feminism*.

CHAPTER I

1. Thomson, *Extraordinary Bodies*, 6.

2. Americans with Disabilities Act of 1990, Public Law 101–336 (July 26, 1990).

3. Bureau of the Census, *Census Brief 97–5* (December 1997).

4. Bureau of the Census, *Press Release CB06-FF.10–2* (July 2006).

5. World Health Organization, *Fact Sheet 135: Population Ageing: A Public Health Challenge* (September 1998).

6. Ibid.

7. See, for example, Smith and Hutchison, *Gendering Disability;* Morris, *Encounters with Strangers;* and Hans and Patri, *Women, Disability and Identity.*

8. Fine and Asch, *Women with Disabilities,* 6. The authors note that race and other identity conditions also add to this experience of handicap.

9. Deegan and Brooks, *Women and Disability.*

10. Stuart and Ellerington, "Unequal Access," 6–17; Fine and Asch, *Women with Disabilities,* 4.

11. Quoted in Stuart and Ellerington, "Unequal Access," 16.

12. Of course, it is important to remember that disabled feminists, as with any other group, hold a wide variety of perspectives and stances.

13. Gartner and Joe, *Images of the Disabled, Disabling Images,* 207.

14. Ruether, *Sexism and God-talk,* 20.

15. Thistlethwaite and Engel, *Lift Every Voice,* 3.

16. Pelka, *Disability Rights Movement,* xii.

17. Stuart, "Disruptive Bodies," 168.

18. For a thorough review of this topic, see Pelka, *Disability Rights Movement,* and Albrecht, Seelman, and Bury, *Handbook of Disability Studies.*

19. These images can be seen from Shakespeare (Richard III) and Melville (Ahab) to Batman (the Joker and Two-Face) and Looney Tunes (Porky Pig and Elmer Fudd). See Gartner and Joe, *Images of the Disabled, Disabling Images,* and Longmore, *Why I Burned My Book and Other Essays on Disability.*

20. *Buck v. Bell,* 274 U.S. 200 (1927).

21. Pelka, *Disability Rights Movement,* 53.

22. Ibid., xi.

23. Ibid. This ordinance was not repealed until 1974. Similar ordinances were also passed in San Francisco, Omaha, and Columbus.

24. *PARC v. Commonwealth of Pennsylvania,* 334 F. Supp. 1257 (1972), established, for the first time, the right of children with disabilities to receive a public education, sparking an explosion of other disability rights litigation.

25. Disability rights activists will be quick, though, to point out the prevalence of portrayals of disability by nondisabled actors, also known as "disability blackface" (e.g., the actor who portrayed the wheelchair-using oldest brother on the television show *Joan of Arcadia* does not use a wheelchair himself). and the emphasis on "acceptable" images of disability, such as people with disabilities who "pass" (e.g., the lead character on *Sue Thomas FBI* was often praised for not appearing Deaf) or who play the stereotypical role of either victim (Jerry's Kids) or "supercrip" (having special powers connected to their disability, as the character of Johnny Smith in *The Dead Zone,* or who are portrayed as triumphing over adversity and being inspirational as a result of their disability, as in any given "movie of the week"). See Nelson, *The Disabled, the Media, and the Information Age.*

26. Thomson, *Extraordinary Bodies,* 5.

27. Snyder, Brueggemann, and Thomson, *Disability Studies,* 2.

28. Wilson and Lewiecki-Wilson, *Embodied Rhetorics,* xi.

29. Davis, *Disability Studies Reader,* 3.

30. Ibid., 2.

31. Gilman, *Disease and Representation;* Rothman, *The Discovery of the Asylum;* Goffman, *Stigma;* Fiedler, *Freaks;* Sontag, *Illness as Metaphor;* Bakhtin, *Rabelais and His World;* Foucault, *The Birth of the Clinic;* Derrida, *Memoirs of the Blind;* Butler, *Bodies That Matter;* and Bordo, *Unbearable Weight.*

32. See McCloughry and Morris, *Making a World of Difference,* 9.

33. Mitchell and Snyder, *The Body and Physical Difference,* 1.

34. Donoghue, "Challenging the Authority of the Medical Definition of Disability," 200.

35. Goffman, *Stigma.*

36. Freidson, "Disability as Social Deviance," 71–99.

37. Eiesland, *Disabled God,* 101.

38. Barton, *Disability and Society,* 13.

39. Pelka, *Disability Rights Movement,* 3.

40. Ibid.

41. It is interesting to note that differing views of self and society have influenced the emergence of the disability rights movement in different locations. See Hurst, "The International Politics of Disability,"18.

42. Charlton, *Nothing about Us without Us,* 3.

43. Ibid., 17.

44. McCloughry and Morris, *Making a World of Difference,* 17.

45. Corker and French, *Disability Discourse,* 2.

46. Ibid., 4.

47. Shildrick, *Leaky Bodies and Boundaries.*

48. Peters, "The Politics of Disability Identity," 215.

49. The capitalized term indicates the culturally Deaf, those who use sign language as their primary form of communication and who identify with the Deaf community, as opposed to the noncapitalized word "deaf," which simply indicates those who experience a loss of hearing.

50. For more information on this perspective, see Branson and Miller, *Damned for Their Difference,* and Bragg, *Deaf World.*

51. Davis, *Disability Studies Reader,* 6.

52. Woodcock, "Cochlear Implants vs. Deaf Culture?" 327.

53. Ibid.

54. Corker and Shakespeare, *Disability/Postmodernity,* 15.

55. Branson and Miller, *Damned for their Difference.,* xiv.

56. This model is a new proposal, but it is in line with demands by figures such as Lennard Davis, Mairian Corker, Tom Shakespeare, and Elizabeth Stuart that disability studies needs an alternative to the existing medical and minority frameworks.

57. Davis, *Enforcing Normalcy,* 1.

58. Stuart, "Disruptive Bodies," 168.

59. It is important to note that limits are not the same as impairment. As argued earlier, the insights of the medical and minority models are still valuable: people with disabilities (or with profound individual and social experiences of limits) are often oppressed, and functional limitations do (at least at times) lead to a diminished quality of life. The limits model instead offers a complementary third approach that questions

individual and societal understandings of normalcy and highlights human limits as appropriate for theoretical and theological reflection.

CHAPTER 2

1. Eiesland, "Barriers and Bridges," 218.
2. Boylan, *Women and Disability*, 16.
3. Kern, *Pastoral Ministry with Disabled Persons*, 181.
4. Jackson, *Conquering Disability*; Moede, *God's Power and Our Weakness*.
5. Webb-Mitchell, *Unexpected Guests at God's Banquet*, 9.
6. For example, a 2000 study by the National Organization on Disability found that people with disabilities are less likely to attend religious studies at least once per month (47 percent) than are people without disabilities (65 percent). The same study suggested that this is not an indication of religious faith, in that 84 percent of people with disabilities and 87 percent of people without disabilities consider religious faith to be important to them. National Organization on Disability, *2000 Survey of Americans with Disabilities*. http://www.nod.org (accessed September 8, 2007).
7. Eiesland, *Disabled God*, 70–71.
8. Ibid.
9. Miles, *The Word Made Flesh*, 1.
10. Important exceptions include Brown, *The Body and Society*; Bynum, *Fragmentation and Redemption*; and Coakley, *Religion and the Body*. The "body craze" mentioned in the introduction to this book is having an impact in historical studies on religious texts and traditions, so it is likely that scholarship in this area will drastically expand in the near future.
11. Miles, *Fullness of Life*, 10.
12. Martin, *Corinthian Body*, 3.
13. Avalos, *Illness and Health Care in the Ancient Near East*, 26.
14. Tan, "The Disabled Christ," 8.
15. Brown, *The Body and Society*, 9.
16. Edwards, "Constructions of Physical Disability in the Ancient Greek World," 36.
17. Brown, *Boundaries of Our Habitations*, 148.
18. Ibid.
19. Ibid., 3.
20. Davaney, *Pragmatic Historicism*, 1.
21. Ibid., 150.
22. See, for example, Wilson and Lewiecki-Wilson, *Embodied Rhetorics*; Snyder, Brueggemann, and Thomson, *Disability Studies*; Schilling, *The Body and Social Theory*; Cohen and Weiss, *Thinking the Limits of the Body*; and Coupland and Gwyn, *Discourse, the Body, and Identity*.
23. For a discussion of some of the various perspectives on the body in non-Christian religious traditions, see Hinnells and Porter, *Religion, Health, and Suffering*; Kinsley, *Health, Healing, and Religion*; Coakley, *Religion and the Body*; Freeman and Abrams, *Illness and Health in the Jewish Tradition*; and Eilberg-Schwartz, *People of the Body*.

24. Important works dealing specifically with a history of disability include Abrams, *Judaism and Disability;* Stiker, *Corps infirmes et sociétés;* Garland, *Eye of the Beholder;* Mitchell and Snyder, *The Body and Physical Difference;* and Covey, *Social Perceptions of People with Disabilities in History.*

25. Brown, *The Body and Society.*

26. These include Bynum, *Holy Feast and Holy Fast,* and Bell, *Holy Anorexia.*

27. See Koenig, McCullough, and Larson, *Handbook of Religion and Health,* 24–52, for a time line of historical understandings of religion, science, and medicine.

28. Ferngren and Amundsen, "Medicine and Religion," 54–55.

29. Stiker, *Corps infirmes et sociétés,* 39, 47ff.; Roccatagliata, *History of Ancient Psychiatry,* 4.

30. See Mauceri, *The Great Break;* Ferngren and Amundsen, "Medicine and Religion"; Edwards, "Constructions of Physical Disability in the Ancient Greek World"; Roccatagliata, *History of Ancient Psychiatry;* Hippocrates, *The Writings of Hippocrates.*

31. Plato, *Phaedo,* 197.

32. Plato, *Phaedrus,* 246ab, 253–254b.

33. Aristotle, *De Anima,* bk. 2, chap. 1.

34. Aristotle, *Generation of Animals,* 4.3.767b, 4.6.775a.

35. Ibid., 4.3.769b.

36. Brown, *The Body and Society,* 9; Martin, *Corinthian Body,* 6.

37. Berquist, *Controlling Corporeality.*

38. See Avalos, *Illness and Health Care in the Ancient Near East,* and Avalos, *Health Care and the Rise of Christianity;* Shuman and Volk, *Reclaiming the Body.*

39. Avalos, *Illness and Health Care in the Ancient Near East,* 235.

40. Deuteronomy 28:27–28, 35, 60–61.

41. Numbers 12:1–16.

42. 2 Samuel 24:10–25.

43. Exodus 15:26.

44. Berquist, *Controlling Corporeality,* 11.

45. Avalos, *Illness and Health Care in the Ancient Near East,* 249.

46. Avalos, *Health Care and the Rise of Christianity,* 37. See also Sawyer, *Reading Leviticus.*

47. Stiker, *Corps infirmes et sociétés,* 24.

48. Ibid., 26.

49. See especially the writings of Elisabeth Schüssler Fiorenza and Phyllis Trible for more on this issue.

50. Ware, "My Helper and My Enemy," 92.

51. Isherwood and Stuart, *Introducing Body Theology,* 11.

52. Tan, "The Disabled Christ," 12.

53. Mark 10:49; Matthew 9:22; Mark 1:41. For more on Jesus and healing, see Epperly, *God's Touch,* and Porterfield, *Healing in the History of Christianity.*

54. Mark 3:1; Luke 13:10–11.

55. Matthew 21:14.

56. Robinson, *The Body,* 9.

57. See Boyarin, *A Radical Jew*, esp. 59–85, for a detailed reading of Paul's positive sensibility toward the body in spite of his Hellenistic-Platonic devaluation of the physical.

58. Roetzel, *The Letters of Paul*.

59. See Ware, "My Helper and My Enemy," 93.

60. Jewett, *Paul's Anthropological Terms*, 458.

61. Galatians 5:19–21.

62. 1 Corinthians 15:35. This interpretation is presented by Isherwood and Stuart, *Introducing Body Theology*, 63.

63. Bultmann, *Theology of the New Testament*, 192.

64. Ibid., 192–193.

65. Brown, *The Body and Society*, 54.

66. Tertullian *De Pudic* xiii.6; *Against Marcion*, bk. V, chap. xii.

67. For a modern summary of these various interpretations, see Sampley, "The Second Letter to the Corinthians," 164–167.

68. Leary, "A Thorn in the Flesh," 520–522.

69. Woods, "Opposition to a Man and His Message," 52.

70. Chrysostom, *Homilies on II Corinthians*, homily XXVI.

71. McCant, "Paul's Thorn of Rejected Apostleship," 551.

72. Russell, "Redemptive Suffering and Paul's Thorn in the Flesh," 565–566.

73. Garrett, "Paul's Thorn and Cultural Models of Affliction," 83.

74. Isherwood and Stuart, *Introducing Body Theology*, 16.

75. For a review of these positions, see Dunnill, "Being a Body," 110.

76. See Avalos, *Health Care and the Rise of Christianity*; Stark, *The Rise of Christianity*; and Stark, "Epidemics, Networks, and the Rise of Christianity."

77. For a more detailed description of this complex period in history, see Bynum, *Fragmentation and Redemption*; Bynum, *The Resurrection of the Body in Western Christianity*; Jantzen, *Power, Gender and Christian Mysticism*; and Biller and Minnis, *Medieval Theology and the Natural Body*.

78. Stuart, "Disruptive Bodies," 169.

79. See Creamer, "Finding God in Our Bodies"; Eiesland, *Disabled God*; and Webb-Mitchell, *Dancing with Disabilities*.

80. See Majik, "Disability for the Religious," 24–25.

81. Block, *Copious Hosting*, 50.

82. Ibid.

83. Ibid., 51.

CHAPTER 3

1. West, "The New Cultural Politics of Difference," 93.

2. See, for example, Foucault, *Power/Knowledge* and *Discipline and Punishment*; Merleau-Ponty, *Phenomenology of Perception*; and MacIntyre, *Dependent Rational Animals*.

3. Saiving, "The Human Situation."

4. Daly, *Beyond God the Father*, 19.

5. Ibid., 9. Daly's views changed drastically only a few years later, when she called for women to abandon patriarchal/institutional Christianity altogether.

6. Ruether, *Sexism and God-talk*, 116, 19.

7. Ibid, 13; italics in original.

8. Cone, *God of the Oppressed*, 15.

9. Gutiérrez, *Theology of Liberation*, xiii.

10. These scholars themselves exhibited universalizing tendencies; their importance here comes from their demand that theology pay attention to experiences of difference.

11. Hull, Scott, and Smith, *All the Women Are White, All the Blacks Are Men, But Some of Us Are Brave.*

12. Some scholars are beginning to attend to disability as a theological issue, either on its own or within the context of other identity concerns. See, for example, the work of Elizabeth Stuart, Doreen Freeman, and myself.

13. For example, as of the time of this writing, there have been no articles on disability in the *Journal of the American Academy of Religion.*

14. Three important exceptions are Ruether, *Gender, Ethnicity, and Religion;* Chopp and Taylor, *Reconstructing Christian Theology;* and Bach, *Women in the Hebrew Bible.*

15. For example, Adams et al., *Readings for Diversity and Social Justice;* Freedman and Holmes, *The Teacher's Body.*

16. McFague, *Body of God*, 108.

17. Nelson, *Body Theology*, 42.

18. Ibid., 50.

19. Isherwood and Stuart, *Introducing Body Theology*, 22.

20. Dunnill, "Being a Body," 110.

21. Griffith, *Born Again Bodies.*

22. Cahill, *Theological Bioethics.*

23. Glucklich, *Sacred Pain.*

24. Althaus-Reid and Isherwood, *The Sexual Theologian;* Pinn and Hopkins, *Loving the Body.*

25. McFague, "An Earthly Theological Agenda," 2.

26. McFague, *Metaphorical Theology*, 143.

27. McFague, *Models of God*, ix.

28. Ibid., 97–180.

29. McFague, *Body of God*, 149.

30. Her reason for identification with the Christian tradition appears to be pragmatic as well—noting that traditional images are often destructive, she seeks to offer alternatives that can benefit the tradition and do less harm. Note, however, that a number of commentators question how well her models actually cohere to the Christian tradition. See, for example, Schrein, *Quilting and Braiding.*

31. McFague, *Body of God*, ix.

32. Ibid., x.

33. For a nuanced description of McFague's criteria for theological adequacy, see McFague, *Body of God*, esp. 13–25; French, "The World as God's Body"; and Davaney, *Pragmatic Historicism*, esp. 90–99.

34. McFague, *Body of God*, vii.

35. Ibid., viii.

36. Ibid., 14.

37. Ibid., viii.

38. Ibid.

39. Ibid.

40. Ibid., vii–viii.

41. Ibid., 16.

42. Ibid., 149.

43. Ibid., ix.

44. Ibid., 211.

45. McFague, *Models of God*, 64, citing Kaufman, *Theology for a Nuclear Age*, 42.

46. McFague, *Models of God*, 65.

47. McFague, *Body of God*, 2–8.

48. Ibid., 7.

49. Ibid., 150.

50. McFague, "Intimate Creation," 42.

51. McFague, *Body of God*, 110.

52. Ibid., 108.

53. Ibid., 182.

54. Ibid., 206.

55. Ibid., 173.

56. Ibid., 174.

57. Ibid., 172.

58. See, for example, Bracken, "Images of God within Systematic Theology"; Schrein, *Quilting and Braiding;* and Chapman, "What God Can Help?"

59. Wells, "The Flesh of God," 58. See also Finger, "Trinity, Ecology and Panentheism."

60. See, for example, Barbour, "Response to Critiques of *Religion in an Age of Science*," 51–65. Barbour worries that, because the cosmos lacks the levels of organization and coordinated communication that McFague seems to imply, her model could revert to a mind/body dualism, where God is the mind and nature is still other. He finds greater promise in process thought. See also Jones, "Women's Experience." Jones notes that McFague's story "leaves little room for a consideration of science's own internally generated epistemic ruptures, gaps, and anomalies" (46).

61. Webb, "Should We Love All of Nature?" See also Palmer, review of *Super, Natural Christians.*

62. McFague, *Life Abundant*, xi–xiv.

63. Nunez, "Can a Christian Environmental Ethic Go Wild?"

64. For more on this critique, see Kwok, "Response to Sallie McFague."

65. Also of interest, but out of the scope of the current project, are critical examinations of McFague's metaphorical approach and her overall methodology. See, for example, Malone, "A Discussion of Sallie McFague's Models of God," (which includes commentary by Kaufman, Ruether, and Tracy); Sontag, "Metaphorical Non-sequitur"; and Davaney, *Pragmatic Historicism*, esp. 90–99. The reader may also be interested in

comparisons between McFague and other major theological figures, including George Lindbeck (see Reynolds, "Walking Apart, Together" and "Parting Company at Last"); Paul Tillich (see Carey, *Paulus Then and Now*); and Jürgen Moltmann (see McWilliams, "Christic Paradigm and Cosmic Christ").

66. See, for example, Carrol, "Models of God or Models of Us?"

67. See Tatman, *Knowledge That Matters*, and Witt, "Epistemology in the Theological Writings of Rosemary Radford Ruether, Sallie McFague, and Carter Heyward."

68. McFague, *Body of God*, 48.

69. Ibid.

70. Ibid., 54; italics in original.

71. Ibid., ix.

72. Clifford, review of *Body of God*, 361.

73. McFague, *Body of God*, viii.

74. Ibid., 175.

75. For example, the experience of cancer may be "chance," but it also draws from genetic and environmental factors. For more on science and chance, see Thistlethwaite, *Adam, Eve, and the Genome*, esp. 52–68 on Mendelian genetics; and Barbour, *Nature, Human Nature, and God*.

76. McFague, *Body of God*, 176.

77. Ibid., 108.

78. Ibid., 113.

79. Ibid., 114.

80. Ibid., 116.

81. Ibid., 121.

82. Ibid., 124.

83. As with any other minority group, however, it is important to recognize that "disability" is not the only category that frames identity, and that "the disabled" include both poor and rich, oppressed and affluent.

84. See Niebuhr, *The Nature and Destiny of Man*. Niebuhr is, of course, not the only one to propose these categories of sin.

85. This lie, for example, would suggest that it is "normal" to look like the cover of a fashion magazine, leading to dangerous body idealization, one factor that contributes to eating disorders and other self-destructive behavior.

86. McFague, *Super, Natural Christians*, 28, quoting Thistlethwaite and Engel, *Lift Every Voice*, 3.

CHAPTER 4

1. Cone, *Black Theology of Liberation*, 1.

2. Gutiérrez, *Theology of Liberation*, xiii.

3. Eiesland, *Disabled God*, 20.

4. Section 307 of the Americans with Disabilities Act of 1990 states, "The provisions of this title shall not apply to private clubs or establishments exempted from coverage under title II of the Civil Rights Act of 1964 (42 U.S.C. 2000-a(e)) or to reli-

gious organizations or entities controlled by religious organizations, including places of worship." This section was an addition to the act as a result of successful lobbying by religious organizations, which argued that full compliance would create an "undue hardship" on their constituents (e.g., it would be too costly to remodel all places of worship) and that the Civil Rights Act of 1964 had set precedence for such an exception.

5. Eiesland, "Barriers and Bridges," 215.

6. Eiesland, *Disabled God*, 67.

7. Ibid., 20.

8. Herzog, "We Have This Ministry," 187.

9. See, for example, National Organization on Disability, *Interfaith Directory of Religious Leaders with Disabilities*. http://www.nod.org (accessed September 8, 2007).

10. Herzog, "We Have This Ministry," 187.

11. Senior, "Beware of the Canaanite Woman," 3.

12. Wilke, *Creating the Caring Congregation*, 30.

13. Block, *Copious Hosting*, 16.

14. This lack is beginning to see remedy, for example, through the creation of the Religion and Disability Studies Group of the American Academy of Religion in 2002.

15. University of Chicago Center on Emergent Disability, "Projects and Reports." http://www.uic.edu/depts/idhd/ced/projects.htm (accessed January 31, 2004).

16. Albrecht, Seelman, and Bury, *Handbook of Disability Studies*, 5.

17. Eiesland, "Encountering the Disabled God," 13.

18. This image of God has similar consequences for people who identify as non-disabled, but it is particularly dangerous to those for whom childlike images are perpetuated in other (nonreligious) ways as well. For example, those who use wheelchairs are often "talked down to" (both literally and figuratively), and those with cognitive disabilities are often treated as children (e.g., assumed to be asexual).

19. Goldberg, *The Changing of the Gods*, 126.

20. Hull, "Blindness and the Face of God," 215.

21. Eiesland, "Liberation, Inclusion, and Justice," 2.

22. See, for example, Webb-Mitchell, "Making the Table Accessible"; Anderson, *Graduate Theological Education and the Human Experience of Disability*; and Herzog, "We Have This Ministry," respectively.

23. Block, *Copious Hosting*, 11.

24. Ibid., 22.

25. Ibid., 91. Block does not explain or support this point but treats it as a self-evident claim.

26. Ibid., 22.

27. Ibid., 120.

28. Ibid., 122–123.

29. Ibid., 143.

30. Black, "The Word Becomes Flesh."

31. Black, *A Healing Homiletic*, 37–38.

32. Ibid., 34.

33. Ibid.

34. Ibid.

35. Ibid., 37.

36. Ibid., 41–42.

37. Ibid., 186.

38. Ibid.

39. Ibid.

40. Ibid.

41. Eiesland, *Disabled God*. Others who have taken up the notion of the Disabled God in significant ways include Fernández, "Jesus Discapacitado"; Willis, "Claiming the 'Fearsome Possibility'"; and Freeman, "A Feminist Theology of Disability."

42. Eiesland, "Things Not Seen," 103.

43. Eiesland, *Disabled God*, 22.

44. Eiesland, "Encountering the Disabled God," 13.

45. Ibid., 14.

46. Chopp, foreword to Eiesland, *Disabled God*, 11.

47. Eiesland, *Disabled God*, 22.

48. Ibid., 94.

49. Ibid., 31.

50. Eiesland's interpretation of the image of Jesus as a person with a disability is primarily metaphorical, but she also argues that real physical disability is apparent in stories of the crucifixion and resurrection.

51. Eiesland, *Disabled God*, 101.

52. Ibid., 86.

53. Eiesland, "What Is Disability?" 28.

54. Ibid., 24.

55. Black and Elkins, *Wising Up*, 39.

56. In a similar vein, there has been very interesting discussion within the Roman Catholic Church about the pope's ability to represent God through a disability. See, for example, Provost, "What If the Pope Became Disabled?".

57. See, for example, Petrella, *Latin American Liberation Theology*.

58. Eiesland, "What Is Disability?" 30.

CHAPTER 5

1. Cohen and Weiss, *Thinking the Limits of the Body*, 2–3.

2. See Derrida, *Margins of Philosophy*, 3–27.

3. Davis, *Enforcing Normalcy*, xiv. Interestingly, many Deaf advocates do not hesitate to classify others as "disabled" using criteria from the medical model, even though such individuals might also reject such labeling themselves.

4. "Ableist" is a political term used by people with disabilities to call attention to assumptions made about normalcy.

5. Davis, *Enforcing Normalcy*, xiv.

6. For a review of signed language structure, see Wilbur, *American Sign Language*.

7. This is counterintuitive for those of us who do hear because we may not even notice that "hard of hearing" references hearing (and Hearing culture). Because "hearing" (including "hard of hearing") is interpreted as different from Deaf, to be called "very hard of hearing" is to be "very different from Deaf."

8. See Black, "The Word Becomes Flesh," 45–51, for more detail on each of these potential differences.

9. An interesting note, which highlights the overlapping structures of identity and minority status, is that, while the abbé's first experience with the Deaf was with girls, he founded a school for boys.

10. See Padden and Humphries, *Deaf in America*, 27–29, for some of the folktales about the abbé. For a detailed history of the development of Deaf language and culture in Europe and America, see Lane, *When the Mind Hears*.

11. Davis, *Enforcing Normalcy*, xiv.

12. Padden and Humphries, *Deaf in America*, 2.

13. Black, "The Word Becomes Flesh," 149.

14. I am using the phrase "cognitive disabilities" in preference to earlier terminology, such as "mental deficiency" or "mental retardation." Other currently accepted terms, some of which will be used by sources that I cite, include "cognitive differences," "intellectual disability," or "developmental delay."

15. See Pelka, *Disability Rights Movement*.

16. See, for example, Foucault's studies of madness and medicine in Foucault, *Madness and Civilization*, and Foucault, *The Birth of the Clinic*.

17. Trent, *Inventing the Feeble Mind*, 2.

18. Davis, *Enforcing Normalcy*, xiii.

19. Ibid., xiv.

20. The same tends to be true for emotional disabilities and mental illness.

21. Prior to January 1, 2007, this organization was known as the American Association on Mental Retardation.

22. American Association on Intellectual and Developmental Disabilities, *Definition of Mental Retardation*. http://www.aamr.org/Policies/faq_mental_retardation.shtml (accessed September 8, 2007).

23. Byrne, *Philosophical and Ethical Problems in Mental Handicap*, 21.

24. Ibid., 22.

25. Goffman, *Asylums*.

26. Wolfensberger, *The Principle of Normalization in Human Services*.

27. Ibid., 13.

28. Trent, *Inventing the Feeble Mind*, 267.

29. Parmenter, "Intellectual Disabilities—Quo Vadis?" 290.

30. Hinkle, "Smart Enough for Church," 2.

31. Ibid.

32. Amos Yong has recently engaged in such a project, but he notes his own struggle as an academic attempting to "translate" or honestly portray these voices and stories. See Yong, *Theology and Down Syndrome*.

33. Webb-Mitchell, *God Plays Piano Too*, 5.

34. Ibid., 14.

35. In addition to the work of Webb-Mitchell, see, for example, Hauerwas, "The Church and Mentally Handicapped Persons," and *Suffering Presence*. For more on the L'Arche movement, see Vanier, *The Challenge of L'Arche*.

36. Eiesland, *Disabled God*, 96.

37. An interesting question would be whether her notion of humanity in fact here becomes a definition of humanity. Do we include people who are not "self-consciously self-conscious," due to cognitive or emotional disability, coma, or even infancy, in the category of "humanity"?

38. McFague, *Body of God*, 100.

39. Welch, interestingly, was herself a student of Sallie McFague, graduating from Vanderbilt in 1982.

40. Welch, *Sweet Dreams in America*, xix.

41. Ibid., 42–43.

42. Ibid., 43.

43. Ibid., xix.

44. McFague, *Models of God*, 3.

45. Eiesland, *Disabled God*, 47.

Bibliography

Abrams, Judith Z. *Judaism and Disability: Portrayals in Ancient Texts from the Tanach through the Bavli.* Washington, DC: Gallaudet University Press, 1998.

Adams, Maurianne, Warren J. Blumenfeld, Rosie Castañeda, Heather W. Hackman, Madeline L. Peters, and Ximena Zíñiga, eds. *Readings for Diversity and Social Justice.* New York: Routledge, 2000.

Albrecht, Gary, Katherine Seelman, and Michael Bury, eds. *Handbook of Disability Studies.* London: Sage, 2001.

Althaus-Reid, Marcella. *From Feminist Theology to Indecent Theology: Readings on Poverty, Sexual identity, and God.* London: SCM Press, 2004.

———. *Indecent Theology: Theological Perversion in Sex, Gender and Politics.* New York: Routledge, 2000.

———, ed. *Liberation Theology and Sexuality.* Aldershot: Ashgate, 2006.

Althaus-Reid, Marcella, and Lisa Isherwood, eds. *The Sexual Theologian: Essays on Sex, God and Politics.* London: T&T Clark, 2004.

Anderson, Robert C., ed., *Graduate Theological Education and the Human Experience of Disability.* Binghamton, NY: Haworth Pastoral Press, 2004.

Avalos, Hector. *Health Care and the Rise of Christianity.* Peabody, MA: Hendrickson, 1999.

———. *Illness and Health Care in the Ancient Near East: The Role of the Temple in Greece, Mesopotamia, and Israel.* Atlanta, GA: Scholars Press, 1995.

Avalos, Hector, Sarah J. Melcher, and Jeremy Schipper, eds. *This Abled Body: Rethinking Disabilities in Biblical Studies.* Atlanta, GA: Society of Biblical Literature, 2007.

Bach, Alice, ed. *Women in the Hebrew Bible: A Reader.* New York: Routledge, 1999.

Bakhtin, Mikhail. *Rabelais and His World*. Bloomington: Indiana University Press, 1984.

Barbour, Ian. *Nature, Human Nature, and God*. Minneapolis: Augsburg Fortress, 2002.

———. "Response to Critiques of *Religion in an Age of Science*." *Zygon* 31 (1996): 51–65.

Bartky, Sandra. "Foreword." In *Men Doing Feminism*, ed. Tom Digby, xi–xiv. New York: Routledge, 1998.

Barton, Len, ed. *Disability and Society: Emerging Issues and Insights*. New York: Longman, 1996.

Beal, Timothy K., and David M. Gunn, eds. *Reading Bibles, Writing Bodies: Identity and the Book*. New York: Routledge, 1997.

Bekkenkamp, Jonneke, and Maaike de Haardt, eds. *Begin with the Body: Corporeality Religion and Gender*. Leuven: Peeters, 1998.

Bell, Rudolph M. *Holy Anorexia*. Chicago: University of Chicago Press, 1985.

Berquist, Jon L. *Controlling Corporeality: The Body and the Household in Ancient Israel*. New Brunswick, NJ: Rutgers University Press, 2002.

Betcher, Sharon V. *Spirit and the Politics of Disablement*. Minneapolis, MN: Fortress Press, 2007.

Betenbaugh, Helen R. "Disability: A Lived Theology." *Theology Today* 57 (2000): 203–210.

———. "Disability and the Canon." Ph.D. diss., Perkins School of Theology, 1997.

Biller, Peter, and A. J. Minnis, eds. *Medieval Theology and the Natural Body*. Rochester, NY: York Medieval Press, 1997.

Bishop, Marilyn, ed. *Religion and Disability: Essays in Scripture, Theology, and Ethics*. Kansas City, MO: Sheed and Ward, 1995.

Black, Kathy. *A Healing Homiletic: Preaching and Disability*. Nashville, TN: Abingdon Press, 1996.

———. *Signs of Solidarity: Ministry with Persons Who Are Deaf, Deafened, and Hard of Hearing*. New York: United Methodist General Board of Global Ministries, 1994.

———. "The Word Becomes Flesh: An Incarnational Model of Preaching Based on Linguistic and Cultural Aspects of the Deaf Community." Ph.D. diss., Graduate Theological Union, 1991.

Black, Kathy, and Heather Murray Elkins, eds. *Wising Up: Ritual Resources for Women of Faith in Their Journey of Aging*. Cleveland, OH: Pilgrim Press, 2005.

Block, Jennie Weiss. *Copious Hosting: A Theology of Access for People with Disabilities*. New York: Continuum, 2002.

Boff, Leonardo, and Clodovis Boff. *Introducing Liberation Theology*. Maryknoll, NY: Orbis Books, 1987

Bordo, Susan. *Unbearable Weight: Feminism, Western Culture, and the Body*. Berkeley: University of California Press, 1993.

Boyarin, Daniel. *A Radical Jew: Paul and the Politics of Identity*. Berkeley: University of California Press, 1994.

Boylan, Esther. *Women and Disability*. London: Zed Books, 1991.

Bracken, Joseph A. "Images of God within Systematic Theology." *Theological Studies* 63 (2002): 362–373.

Bragg, Lois, ed. *Deaf World: A Historical Reader and Primary Sourcebook*. New York: New York University Press, 2001.

Branson, Jan, and Don Miller. *Damned for Their Difference: The Cultural Construction of Deaf People as Disabled*. Washington, DC: Gallaudet University Press, 2002.

Bredberg, Elizabeth. "Writing Disability History: Problems, Perspectives and Sources." *Disability and Society* 14 (1999): 189–201.

Briggs, Sheila. "The Politics of Identity and the Politics of Interpretation." *Union Seminary Quarterly Review* 43 (1989): 163–180.

Brook, Barbara. *Feminist Perspectives on the Body*. New York: Longman, 1999.

Brown, Delwin. *Boundaries of Our Habitations: Tradition and Theological Construction*. Albany: State University of New York Press, 1994.

Brown, Peter. *The Body and Society: Men, Women and Sexual Renunciation in Early Christianity*. New York: Columbia University Press, 1988.

Browne, Susan, ed. *With the Power of Each Breath: A Disabled Women's Anthology*. Pittsburgh: Cleis Press, 1985.

Brueggemann, Brenda Jo. *Lend Me Your Ear: Rhetorical Constructions of Deafness*. Washington, DC: Gallaudet University Press, 1999.

Bultmann, Rudolf. *Theology of the New Testament*. London: SMC Press, 1952.

Butler, Judith P. *Bodies That Matter: On the Discursive Limits of Sex*. New York: Routledge, 1993.

———. *Gender Trouble: Feminism and the Subversion of Identity*. New York: Routledge, 1990.

Butler, Ruth, and Hester Parr, eds. *Mind and Body Spaces: Geographies of Illness, Impairment, and Disability*. New York: Routledge, 1999.

Bynum, Caroline Walker. *Fragmentation and Redemption: Essays on Gender and the Human Body in Medieval Religion*. New York: Zone Books, 1991.

———. *Holy Feast and Holy Fast: The Religious Significance of Food to Medieval Women*. Berkeley: University of California Press, 1987.

———. *The Resurrection of the Body in Western Christianity, 200–1336*. New York: Columbia University Press, 1995.

Bynum, Caroline Walker, Stevan Harrell, and Paula Richman, eds. *Gender and Religion: On the Complexity of Symbols*. Boston: Beacon Press, 1986.

Byrne, Peter. *Philosophical and Ethical Problems in Mental Handicap*. New York: St. Martin's Press, 2000.

Cahill, Lisa Sowle. *Theological Bioethics: Participation, Justice, and Change*. Washington, DC: Georgetown University Press, 2005.

Camporesi, Piero. *The Incorruptible Flesh: Bodily Mutilation and Mortification in Religion and Folklore*. New York: Cambridge University Press, 1988.

Carey, John C. *Paulus Then and Now*. Macon, GA: Mercer University Press, 2002.

Carroll, B. Jill. "Models of God or Models of Us? On the Theology of Sallie McFague." *Encounter* 52 (1991): 183–196.

Chapman, C. Clarke. "What God Can Help? Trinity and Pop Religions of Crisis." *Cross Currents* 44 (1994): 316–331.

Charlton, James I. *Nothing about Us without Us: Disability Oppression and Empowerment.* Berkeley: University of California Press, 1998.

Chopp, Rebecca S., and Sheila Greeve Davaney, eds. *Horizons in Feminist Theology:
Identity, Tradition, and Norms.* Minneapolis: Fortress Press, 1997.

Chopp, Rebecca S., and Mark Lewis Taylor, eds. *Reconstructing Christian Theology.*
Minneapolis: Fortress Press, 1994.

Clifford, Anne. Review of *The Body of God,* by Sallie McFague. *Horizons* 21 (1994): 361.

Coakley, Sarah, ed. *Religion and the Body.* Cambridge: Cambridge University Press,
1997.

Cohen, Jeffrey Jerome, and Gail Weiss, eds. *Thinking the Limits of the Body.* Albany:
State University of New York Press, 2003.

Colston, Lowell G. *Pastoral Care with Handicapped Persons.* Philadelphia: Fortress
Press, 1978.

Cone, James H. *A Black Theology of Liberation.* 2d ed. Maryknoll, NY: Orbis Books, 1986.
———. *God of the Oppressed.* San Francisco: Harper and Row, 1975.

Cooey, Paula M. *Religious Imagination and the Body: A Feminist Analysis.* Oxford: Oxford
University Press, 1994.

Cooey, Paula M., Sharon A. Farmer, and Mary Ellen Ross, eds. *Embodied Love: Sensuality and Relationship as Feminist Values.* San Francisco: Harper and Row, 1987.

Cooper, Burton Z. "The Disabled God: Understanding God's Creative and Redemptive
Love." *Theology Today* 49 (1992): 173–182.

Corker, Mairian. *Deaf and Disabled, or Deafness Disabled?* Philadelphia: Open University Press, 1998.

Corker, Mairian, and Sally French, eds. *Disability Discourse.* Philadelphia: Open University Press, 1999.

Corker, Mairian, and Tom Shakespeare, eds. *Disability/Postmodernity: Embodying Disability Theory.* New York: Continuum, 2002.

Cornell, Drucilla. *The Philosophy of the Limit.* New York: Routledge, 1992

Coupland, Justine, and Richard Gwyn, eds. *Discourse, the Body, and Identity.* New York:
Palgrave Macmillan, 2003.

Covey, Herbert C. *Social Perceptions of People with Disabilities in History.* Springfield, IL:
Thomas, 1998.

Creamer, Deborah. "Finding God in Our Bodies: Theology from the Perspective of People with Disabilities." *Journal of Religion in Disability and Rehabilitation* 2 (1995):
27–42, 67–87.

———. "The Future of Disability in the Teaching of Religion: Views from the Next
Generation." *Spotlight on Teaching/Religious Studies News* 20, no. 3 (2005): xii.

———. " 'God Doesn't Treat His Children That Way': The Experience of Disability in
the Families of God." *Journal of Religion, Disability, and Health* 9, no. 3 (2005):
73–84.

———. "Including All Bodies in the Body of God: Disability and the Theology of Sallie
McFague." *Journal of Religion, Disability, and Health* 9, no. 4 (2005): 55–69.

———. "Theological Accessibility: The Contribution of Disability." *Disability Studies
Quarterly* 26, no. 4 (2006). www.dsq-sds.org.

———. "Toward a Theology That Includes the Human Experience of Disability." In *Graduate Theological Education and the Human Experience of Disability*, ed. Robert C. Anderson, 57–67. Binghamton, NY: Haworth Press, 2003.

———. "What It Means to Be 'Disabled': Ethical and Theological Reflections." *Journal of Lutheran Ethics* 7, no. 7 (2007). www.elca.org/jle.

———. "The Withered Hand of God: Disability and Theological Reflection." Ph.D. diss., Iliff School of Theology and the University of Denver, 2004.

Daly, Mary. *Beyond God the Father: Toward a Philosophy of Women's Liberation*. Boston: Beacon Press, 1973.

Davaney, Sheila Greeve. *Pragmatic Historicism: A Theology for the Twenty-first Century*. Albany: State University of New York Press, 2000.

Davis, Kathy, ed. *Embodied Practices: Feminist Perspectives on the Body*. London: Sage, 1997.

Davis, Lennard J. *Bending Over Backwards: Disability, Dismodernism, and Other Difficult Positions*. New York: New York University Press, 2002.

———, ed. *Disability Studies Reader*. New York: Routledge, 1997.

———. *Enforcing Normalcy: Disability, Deafness, and the Body*. London: Verso, 1995.

Deegan, Mary Jo, and Nancy A. Brooks, eds. *Women and Disability: The Double Handicap*. New Brunswick, NJ: Transaction Books, 1985.

Deland, Jane S. "Images of God through the Lens of Disability." *Journal of Religion, Disability and Health* 3, no. 2 (1999): 47–81.

Derrida, Jacques. *Margins of Philosophy*. Chicago: University of Chicago Press, 1982.

———. *Memoirs of the Blind*. Chicago: University of Chicago Press, 1993.

DeVries, Dawn. "Creation, Handicappism, and the Community of Differing Abilities." In *Reconstructing Christian Theology*, ed. Rebecca S. Chopp and Mark Lewis Taylor, 124–140. Minneapolis, MN: Fortress Press, 1994.

Digby, Tom, ed. *Men Doing Feminism*. New York: Routledge, 1998.

Donoghue, Christopher. "Challenging the Authority of the Medical Definition of Disability." *Disability and Society* 18 (2003): 199–208.

Douglas, Mary. *In The Wilderness: The Doctrine of Defilement in the Book of Numbers*. Sheffield, UK: Sheffield Academic Press, 1993.

———. *Purity and Danger: An Analysis of Concepts of Pollution and Taboo*. London: Routledge and Kegan Paul, 1966.

Dunnill, John. "Being a Body." *Theology* 105 (2002): 110–117.

Edwards, Martha L. "Constructions of Physical Disability in the Ancient Greek World." In *The Body and Physical Difference: Discourses of Disability*, ed. David T. Mitchell and Sharon L. Snyder, 35–50. Ann Arbor: University of Michigan Press, 1997.

Eiesland, Nancy L. "Barriers and Bridges: Relating the Disability Rights Movement and Religious Organizations." In *Human Disability and the Service of God: Reassessing Religious Practice*, ed. Nancy Eiesland and Don E. Saliers, 200–229. Nashville, TN: Abingdon Press, 1998.

———. *The Disabled God: Toward a Liberatory Theology of Disability*. Nashville, TN: Abingdon Press, 1994.

———. "Encountering the Disabled God." *The Other Side* 38, no. 5 (2002): 10–15.

————. "Liberation, Inclusion, and Justice: A Faith Response to Persons with Disabilities." *Impact* 14 (2001): 2–3, 35.

————. "Things Not Seen: Women with Physical Disabilities." In *Liberating Faith Practices: Feminist Practical Theologies in Context*, ed. Denise Ackermann and Reit Bons-Storm, 103–127. Leuven: Peeters, 1998.

————. "What Is Disability?" *Stimulus* 6, no. 4 (1998): 24–25.

Eiesland, Nancy L., and Don E. Saliers, eds. *Human Disability and the Service of God: Reassessing Religious Practice*. Nashville, TN: Abingdon Press, 1998.

Eilberg-Schwartz, Howard. *God's Phallus: And Other Problems for Men and Monotheism*. Boston: Beacon Press, 1994.

————, ed. *People of the Body: Jews and Judaism from an Embodied Perspective*. Albany: State University of New York Press, 1992.

————. *The Savage in Judaism*. Bloomington: Indiana University Press, 1990.

Ellison, Marvin M., and Sylvia Thorson-Smith, eds. *Body and Soul: Rethinking Sexuality as Justice-Love*. Cleveland, OH: Pilgrim Press, 2003.

Elshout, Elly, ed. "Women with Disabilities: A Challenge to Feminist Theology." *Journal of Feminist Studies in Religion* 10 (1994): 99–134

Epperly, Bruce G. *God's Touch: Faith, Wholeness, and the Healing Miracles of Jesus*. Louisville, KY: Westminster John Knox Press, 2001.

Fawcett, Barbara. *Feminist Perspectives on Disability*. New York: Pearson Education, 2000.

Fernández, Noel. "Jesus Discapacitado." *Echos* 19 (2001): 16–17.

Ferngren, Gary B., and Darrel W. Amundsen. "Medicine and Religion: Pre-Christian Antiquity." In *Health/Medicine and the Faith Traditions: An Inquiry into Religion and Medicine*, ed. Martin E. Marty and Kenneth L. Vaux, 53–92. Philadelphia: Fortress Press, 1982.

Fiedler, Leslie. *Freaks: Myths and Images of the Secret Self*. New York: Simon and Schuster, 1978.

Fine, Michelle, and Adrienne Asch, eds. *Women with Disabilities: Essays in Psychology, Culture, and Politics*. Philadelphia: Temple University Press, 1988.

Finger, Thomas. "Trinity, Ecology and Panentheism." *Christian Scholars Review* 27 (1997): 74–98.

Fontaine, Carole R. "Disabilities and Illness in the Bible: A Feminist Perspective." In *A Feminist Companion to the Hebrew Bible in the New Testament*, ed. Althalya Brenner, 286–300. Sheffield, UK: Sheffield Academic Press, 1996.

Foucault, Michel. *The Birth of the Clinic: An Archaeology of Medical Perception*. New York: Pantheon Books, 1973.

————. *Discipline and Punishment*. New York: Pantheon Books, 1977.

————. *Madness and Civilization: A History of Insanity in the Age of Reason*. New York: Pantheon Books, 1965.

————. *Power/Knowledge*. New York: Pantheon Books, 1980.

Freedman, Diane P., and Martha Stoddart Holmes, eds. *The Teacher's Body: Embodiment, Authority, and Identity in the Academy*. Albany: State University of New York Press, 2003.

Freeman, David L., and Judith Z. Abrams, eds. *Illness and Health in the Jewish Tradition: Writings from the Bible to Today*. Philadelphia: Jewish Publication Society, 1999.

Freeman, Doreen. "A Feminist Theology of Disability." *Feminist Theology* 29 (2002): 71–85.

Freidson, Eliot. "Disability as Social Deviance." In *Sociology and Rehabilitation*, ed. Marvin Sussman, 71–99. New York: Arno Press, 1965.

French, William C. "The World as God's Body: Theological Ethics and Panentheism." In *Broken and Whole: Essays on Religion and the Body*, ed. Maureen A. Tilley and Susan A. Ross, 135–144. Lanham, MD: University Press of America, 1993.

Gallagher, Catherine, and Thomas Laqueur, eds. *Making of the Modern Body: Sexuality and Society in the Nineteenth Century*. Berkeley: University of California Press, 1987.

Gallop, Jane. *Thinking through the Body*. New York: Columbia University Press, 1988.

Garland, Robert. *Eye of the Beholder: Deformity and Disability in the Graeco-Roman World*. Ithaca, NY: Cornell University Press, 1995.

Garrett, Susan R. "Paul's Thorn and Cultural Models of Affliction." In *The Social World of the First Christians: Essays in Honor of Wayne A. Meeks*, ed. L. Michael White and O. Larry Yarbrough, 82–99. Minneapolis, MN: Augsburg Fortress, 1995.

Gartner, Alan, and Tom Joe, eds. *Images of the Disabled, Disabling Images*. New York: Praeger, 1987.

Gilman, Sander. *Disease and Representation: Images of Illness from Madness to AIDS*. Ithaca, NY: Cornell University Press, 1988.

Glucklich, Ariel. *Sacred Pain: Hurting the Body for the Sake of the Soul*. Oxford: Oxford University Press, 2001.

Goffman, Erving. *Asylums: Essays on the Social Situation of Mental Patients and Other Inmates*. Chicago: Aldine, 1961.

———. *Stigma: Notes on the Management of Spoiled Identity*. Englewood Cliffs, NJ: Prentice-Hall, 1963.

Goldberg, Naomi. *The Changing of the Gods: Feminism and the End of Traditional Religions*. Boston: Beacon Press, 1979.

Govig, Stewart D. *Strong at the Broken Places: Persons with Disabilities and the Church*. Louisville, KY: Westminster John Knox Press, 1989.

Grantley, Darryll, and Nina Taunton. *The Body in Late Medieval and Early Modern Culture*. Aldershot: Ashgate, 2000

Griffith, R. Marie. *Born Again Bodies: Flesh and Spirit in American Christianity*. Berkeley: University of California Press, 2004.

Grosz, Elizabeth. *Volatile Bodies: Toward a Corporeal Feminism*. Bloomington: Indiana University Press, 1994.

Gutiérrez, Gustavo. *A Theology of Liberation*. Rev. ed. Maryknoll, NY: Orbis Books, 1988.

Hancock, Philip, ed. *The Body, Culture, and Society: An Introduction*. Philadelphia: Open University Press, 2000.

Hannaford, Robert, and J'annine Jobling, eds. *Theology and the Body: Gender, Text and Ideology*. Herefordshire, UK: Gracewing, 1999.

Hans, Asha, and Annie Patri, eds. *Women, Disability and Identity*. Thousand Oaks, CA: Sage, 2003.

Harris, Jennifer. *The Cultural Meaning of Deafness*. Brookfield, VT: Avebury, 1995.

Hauerwas, Stanley. "The Church and Mentally Handicapped Persons: A Continuing Challenge to the Imagination." In *Religion and Disability*, ed. Marilyn Bishop, 46–64. Kansas City: Sheed and Ward, 1995.

———. *Suffering Presence: Theological Reflections on Medicine, the Mentally Handicapped, and the Church*. Notre Dame, IN: University of Notre Dame Press, 1986.

Hawthorne, Gerald, and Ralph Martin, eds. *Dictionary of Paul and His Letters*. Downers Grove, IL: Intervarsity Press, 1993.

Herzog, Albert. "We Have This Ministry: Ordained Ministers Who Are Physically Disabled." In *Human Disability and the Service of God: Reassessing Religious Practice*, ed. Nancy Eiesland and Don Saliers, 187–199. Nashville, TN: Abingdon Press, 1998.

Hillyer, Barbara. *Feminism and Disability*. Norman: University of Oklahoma Press, 1993.

Hinkle, Christopher. "Smart Enough for Church." Paper presented at the annual meeting of the American Academy of Religion, Atlanta, Georgia, November 2003.

Hinnells, John R., and Roy Porter, eds. *Religion, Health, and Suffering*. London: Kegan Paul, 1999.

Hippocrates. *The Writings of Hippocrates: The Epidemic*. Franklin Center, PA: Franklin Library, 1979.

Holden, Lynn. *Forms of Deformity*. Sheffield, UK: Sheffield Academic Press, 1991.

hooks, bell. *Feminist Theory: From Margin to Center*. Boston: South End Press, 1984.

Horner, Avril, and Angela Keane, eds. *Body Matters: Feminism, Textuality, Corporeality*. Manchester, UK: Manchester University Press, 2000.

Hull, Gloria T., Patricia Bell Scott, and Barbara Smith, eds. *All the Women Are White, All the Blacks Are Men, But Some of Us Are Brave*. Old Westbury, NY: Feminist Press, 1982.

Hull, John M. "Blindness and the Face of God: Toward a Theology of Disability." In *The Human Image of God*, ed. Hans-Georg Ziebertz et al., 215–229. Leiden: Brill, 2001.

Hurst, Rachel. "The International Politics of Disability." *Transformation* 15, no. 4 (1998): 17–19.

Isherwood, Lisa, ed. *Good News of the Body: Sexual Theology and Feminism*. New York: New York University Press, 2000.

Isherwood, Lisa, and Elizabeth Stuart. *Introducing Body Theology*. Sheffield, UK: Sheffield Academic Press, 1998.

Iwakuma, Miho. "The Body as Embodiment." In *Disability/Postmodernity: Embodying Disability Theory*, ed. Mairian Corker and Tom Shakespeare, 76–87. New York: Continuum, 2002.

Jackson. Edgar. *Conquering Disability*. Minneapolis, MN: Augsburg Fortress, 1989.

Jaggar, Alison M., and Susan R. Bordo, eds. *Gender/Body/Knowledge: Feminist Reconstructions of Being and Knowing*. New Brunswick, NJ: Rutgers University Press, 1989.

Jantzen, Grace M. *God's World, God's Body*. Philadelphia: Westminster Press, 1984.

———. *Power, Gender, and Christian Mysticism*. Cambridge: Cambridge University Press, 1995.

Jardine, Alice, and Paul Smith, eds. *Men in Feminism*. New York: Methuen, 1987.

Jensen, David H. *In the Company of Strangers*. Cleveland, OH: Pilgrim Press, 2001.

Jewett, Robert. *Paul's Anthropological Terms*. Leiden: Brill, 1971.

Johnstone, Albert A. "The Bodily Nature of the Self." In *Giving the Body Its Due*, ed. Maxine Sheets-Johnstone, 16–47. Albany: State University of New York Press, 1992.

Jones, Serene. "Women's Experience: Between a Rock and a Hard Place." In *Horizons in Feminist Theology: Identity, Tradition, and Norms*, ed. Rebecca Chopp and Sheila Greeve Davaney, 33–53. Minneapolis, MN: Fortress Press, 1997.

Kaufman, Gordon. "Nuclear Eschatology and the Study of Religion." *Journal of the American Academy of Religion* 51 (1983): 3–14.

———. *Theology for a Nuclear Age*. Philadelphia: Westminster Press, 1985.

Keenan, James F. "Christian Perspectives on the Human Body." *Theological Studies* 55 (1994): 330–346.

Kern, Walter. *Pastoral Ministry with Disabled Persons*. New York: Alba House, 1985.

Kim, C.W. Maggie, Susan M. St. Ville, and Susan M. Simonaitis, eds. *Transfigurations: Theology and the French Feminists*. Minneapolis, MN: Augsburg Fortress, 1993.

King, Karen, ed. *Images of the Feminine in Gnosticism*. Philadelphia: Fortress Press, 1988.

———. *What Is Gnosticism?* Cambridge, MA: Harvard University Press, 2003.

Kinsley, David. *Health, Healing, and Religion: A Cross-Cultural Perspective*. Upper Saddle River, NJ: Prentice-Hall, 1996.

Koenig, Harold G., Michael E. McCullough, and David B. Larson, eds. *Handbook of Religion and Health*. Oxford: Oxford University Press, 2001.

Komesaroff, Paul A., ed. *Troubled Bodies: Critical Perspectives on Postmodernism, Medical Ethics, and the Body*. Durham, NC: Duke University Press, 1995.

Krafft, Jane. *Ministry to Persons with Disabilities*. Collegeville, MN: Liturgical Press, 1988.

Kwok Pui-Lan. "Response to Sallie McFague." In *Christianity and Ecology*, ed. Dieter T. Hessel and Rosemary Radford Ruether, 47–50. Cambridge, MA: Harvard University Center for the Study of World Religions, 2000.

Lane, Harlan L. *When the Mind Hears: A History of the Deaf*. New York: Vintage Books, 1989.

Lane, Nancy J. "A Theology of Anger When Living with Disability." *Rehabilitation Education* 9 (1995): 97–111.

Law, Jane Marie, ed. *Religious Reflections on the Human Body*. Bloomington: Indiana University Press, 1995.

Layton, Richard A. *Didymus the Blind and His Circle in Late-Antique Alexandria: Virtue and Narrative in Biblical Scholarship*. Urbana: University of Illinois Press, 2004.

Leary, T. J. "A Thorn in the Flesh." *Journal of Theological Studies* 43 (1992): 520–522.

Ledure, Yves. *Transcendances: Essai sur Dieu et le corps*. Paris: Desclee de Brouwer, 1989.

Lewis, Hannah. *Deaf Liberation Theology*. Aldershot: Ashgate, 2007.

Linscheid, John. "Disability Rights: Transforming Our Views of Ability." *The Other Side* 22, no. 2 (1986): 48.

Llewellyn, A., and K. Hogan. "The Use and Abuse of Models of Disability." *Disability and Society* 15 (2000): 157–165.

Longhurst, Robyn. *Bodies: Exploring Fluid Boundaries*. London: Routledge, 2001.

Longmore, Paul K. *Why I Burned My Book and Other Essays on Disability*. Philadelphia: Temple University Press, 2003.

Lonsdale, Susan. *Women and Disability: The Experience of Physical Disability among Women*. New York: St. Martin's Press, 1990.

Louth, Andrew. "The Body in Western Catholic Christianity." In *Religion and the Body*, ed. Sarah Coakley, 111–130. Cambridge: Cambridge University Press, 1997.

MacIntyre, Alasdair. *Dependent Rational Animals: Why Human Beings Need the Virtues*. Chicago: Open Court, 1999.

Majik, P. J. "Disability for the Religious." *Disability Rag and Resource* 15 (1994): 24–25.

Malone, Nancy, ed. "A Discussion of Sallie McFague's Models of God." *Religion and Intellectual Life* 5 (1988): 9–44.

Marks, Deborah. *Disability: Controversial Debates and Psychosocial Perspectives*. New York: Routledge, 1999.

Martin, Dale. *The Corinthian Body*. New Haven, CT: Yale University Press, 1995.

Marty, Martin E., and Kenneth L. Vaux, eds. *Health/Medicine and the Faith Traditions: An Inquiry into Religion and Medicine*. Philadelphia: Fortress Press, 1982.

Mauceri, Joseph. *The Great Break: A Short History of the Separation of Medical Science from Religion*. Barrytown, NY: Station Hill Press, 1986.

McCant, Jerry W. "Paul's Thorn of Rejected Apostleship." *New Testament Studies* 34 (1988): 550–572.

McCloughry, Roy, and Wayne Morris. *Making a World of Difference: Christian Reflections on Disability*. London: SPCK, 2002.

McCutcheon, Russell T. *Critics Not Caretakers: Redescribing the Public Study of Religion*. Albany: State University of New York Press, 2001.

McFague, Sallie. *The Body of God: An Ecological Theology*. Minneapolis, MN: Fortress Press, 1993.

———. "Cosmology and Christianity: Implications of the Common Creation Story for Theology." In *Theology at the End of Modernity*, ed. Sheila Greeve Davaney, 19–40. Philadelphia: Trinity Press, 1991.

———. "An Earthly Theological Agenda." *Christian Century* 108 (1991): 12–15.

———. "Human Beings, Embodiment, and Our Home the Earth." In *Reconstructing Christian Theology*, ed. Rebecca S. Chopp and Mark Lewis Taylor, 141–169. Minneapolis, MN: Fortress Press, 1994.

———. "Intimate Creation: God's Body, Our Home." *Christian Century* 119, no. 6 (2002): 42.

———. "Is God in Charge?" In *Essentials of Christian Theology*, ed. William C. Placher, 101–116. Louisville, KY: Westminster John Knox Press, 2003.

———. *Life Abundant: Rethinking Theology and Economy for a Planet in Peril*. Minneapolis, MN: Fortress Press, 2001.

————. *Literature and the Christian Life*. New Haven, CT: Yale University Press, 1966.

————. "The Loving Eye vs. the Arrogant Eye: Christian Critique of the Western Gaze on Nature and the Third World." *Ecumenical Review* 49 (1997): 185–193.

————. *Metaphorical Theology: Models of God in Religious Language*. Philadelphia: Fortress Press, 1982.

————. *Models of God: Theology for an Ecological, Nuclear Age*. Philadelphia: Fortress Press, 1987.

————. *A New Climate for Theology: God, the World, and Global Warming*. Minneapolis, MN: Fortress Press, 2008.

————. *Speaking in Parables: A Study in Metaphor and Theology*. Philadelphia: Fortress Press, 1975.

————. *Super, Natural Christians: How We Should Love Nature*. Minneapolis, MN: Fortress Press, 1997.

————. "The Theologian as Advocate." *Theological Education* 25 (1989): 79–97.

————. "The World as God's Body." *Christian Century* 105 (1998): 671–673.

McLeod, Frederick G. "The Antiochene Tradition Regarding the Role of the Body within the Image of God." In *Broken and Whole: Essays on Religion and the Body*, ed. Maureen A. Tilley and Susan A. Ross, 23–53. Lanham, MD: University Press of America, 1993.

McRuer, Robert. *Crip Theory: Cultural Signs of Queerness and Disability*. New York: New York University Press, 2006.

McTernan, Vaughn. Review *of Super, Natural Christians*, by Sallie McFague. *Zygon* (35): 995–996.

McWilliams, Warren. "Christic Paradigm and Cosmic Christ: Ecological Christology in the Theologies of Sallie McFague and Jurgen Moltmann." *Perspectives in Religious Studies* 25 (1998): 341–355.

Merleau-Ponty, Maurice. *Phenomenology of Perception*. New York: Routledge, 1962.

Miles, M. "Disability in an Eastern Religious Context: Historical Perspectives." *Disability and Society* 10 (1995): 49–70.

Miles, Margaret R. *Augustine on the Body*. Missoula, MT: Scholars Press, 1979.

————. "Carnal Abominations: The Female Body as Grotesque." In *The Grotesque in Art and Literature: Theological Reflections*, ed. James Luther Adams and Wilson Yates, 83–112. Grand Rapids, MI: Eerdmans, 1997.

————. *Carnal Knowing: Female Nakedness and Religious Meaning in the Christian West*. New York: Vintage Books, 1991.

————. *Fullness of Life: Historical Foundations for a New Asceticism*. Philadelphia: Westminster Press, 1981.

————. *Plotinus on Body and Beauty: Society, Philosophy, and Religion in Third-Century Rome*. Oxford: Blackwell, 1999.

————. *Practicing Christianity: Critical Perspectives for an Embodied Spirituality*. New York: Crossroad, 1988.

————. "Revisioning an Embodied Christianity." *Unitarian Universalist Christian* 42 (1987): 5–13.

————. *The Word Made Flesh: A History of Christian Thought*. Malden, MA: Blackwell, 2005.

Mitchell, David T., and Sharon L. Snyder, eds. *The Body and Physical Difference: Discourses of Disability*. Ann Arbor: University of Michigan Press, 1997.

Moede, Gerald, ed. *God's Power and Our Weakness*. Princeton, NJ: Consultation on Church Union, 1982.

Mohrmann, Margaret E., and Mark J. Hanson, eds. *Pain Seeking Understanding: Suffering, Medicine, and Faith*. Cleveland, OH: Pilgrim Press, 1999.

Moltmann-Wendel, Elisabeth. *I Am My Body: A Theology of Embodiment*. New York: Continuum, 1995.

Moore, Stephen. *God's Gym: Divine Male Bodies of the Bible*. New York: Routledge, 1996.

Morris, Jenny, ed., *Encounters with Strangers: Feminism and Disability*. London: Women's Press, 1999.

Nelson, J. Robert. "Challenging Disabled Theology." *Christian Century* 98 (1981): 1244–1245.

Nelson, Jack A., ed. *The Disabled, the Media, and the Information Age*. Westport, CT: Greenwood Press, 1994.

Nelson, James B. *Body Theology*. Louisville, KY: Westminster John Knox Press, 1992.

Niebuhr, Reinhold. *The Nature and Destiny of Man*. New York: Scribner's, 1941.

Nunez, Theodore. "Can a Christian Environmental Ethic Go Wild? Evaluating Eco-theological Responses to the Wilderness Debate." *Annual of the Society of Christian Ethics* 20 (2000): 329–348.

Nussbaum, Martha C. *The Therapy of Desire: Theory and Practice in Hellenistic Ethics*. Princeton, NJ: Princeton University Press, 1994.

Oliver, Michael. *Understanding Disability: From Theory to Practice*. New York: St. Martin's Press, 1996.

Padden, Carol, and Tom Humphries. *Deaf in America: Voices from a Culture*. Cambridge, MA: Harvard University Press, 1988.

Pailin, David A. *A Gentle Touch: From a Theology of Handicap to a Theology of Human Being*. London: SPCK, 1992.

Palmer, Clare. Review of *Body of God*, by Sallie McFague. *Feminist Theology* 8 (1995): 123–125.

————. Review of *Super, Natural Christians*, by Sallie McFague. *Journal of Theological Studies* 49 (1998): 922–924.

Parel, Kamala. "The Disease of the Passions in Clement of Alexander." *Studia Patristica XXXVI*, 449–455. Louvain: Peeters, 2001.

Parmenter, Trevor. "Intellectual Disabilities—Quo Vadis?" In *Handbook of Disability Studies*, ed. Gary Albrecht, Katherine Seelman, and Michael Bury, 267–296. London: Sage, 2001.

Pelka, Fred. *The Disability Rights Movement*. Santa Barbara, CA: ABC-CLIO, 1997.

Perkins, Judith. *The Suffering Self: Pain and Narrative Representation in the Early Christian Era*. New York: Routledge, 1995.

Peters, Susan. "The Politics of Disability Identity." In *Disability and Society: Emerging Issues and Insights*, ed. Len Barton, 215–234. New York: Longman, 1996.

Petrella, Ivan, ed. *Latin American Liberation Theology: The Next Generation*. Maryknoll, NY: Orbis Books, 2005.

Pilch, John J. *Healing in the New Testament: Insights from Medical and Mediterranean Anthropology*. Minneapolis, MN: Fortress Press, 2000.

Pinn, Anthony B., and Dwight N. Hopkins, eds. *Loving the Body: Black Religious Studies and the Erotic*. New York: Palgrave Macmillan, 2004.

Porterfield, Amanda. *Healing in the History of Christianity*. Oxford: Oxford University Press, 2005

Price, Janet, and Margrit Shildrick, eds. *Feminist Theory and the Body: A Reader*. New York: Routledge, 1999.

Prokes, Mary Timothy. *Toward a Theology of the Body*. Edinburgh: T&T Clark, 1996.

Prosser, Diane Louise. *Transgressive Corporeality: The Body, Poststructuralism, and the Theological Imagination*. Albany: State University of New York Press, 1995.

Provost, James H. "What If the Pope Became Disabled?" *America* 183, no. 9 (2000): 7–9.

Raphael, Melissa. *Thealogy and Embodiment: The Post-patriarchal Reconstruction of Female Sacrality*. Sheffield, UK: Sheffield Academic Press, 1996.

Reinders, Hans S. *Receiving the Gift of Friendship: Profound Disability, Theological Anthropology, and Ethics*. Grand Rapids, MI: Eerdmans, 2008.

Reynolds, Terrence. "Parting Company at Last: Lindbeck and McFague in Substantive Theological Dialogue." *Concordia Theological Quarterly* 63 (1999): 97–118.

———. "Two McFagues: Meaning, Truth, and Justification in Models of God." *Modern Theology* 11 (1995): 289–313.

———. "Walking Apart, Together: Lindbeck and McFague on Theological Method." *Journal of Religion* 77 (1997): 44–67.

Reynolds, Thomas E. *Vulnerable Communion: A Theology of Disability and Hospitality*. Grand Rapids, MI: Brazos Press, 2008.

Robinson, John A.T. *The Body: A Study in Pauline Theology*. Chicago: Henry Regnery, 1952.

Roccatagliata, Giuseppe. *A History of Ancient Psychiatry*. New York: Greenwood Press, 1986.

Roetzel, Calvin. *The Letters of Paul: Conversations in Context*. Louisville, KY: Westminster John Knox Press, 1998.

Rothman, David. *The Discovery of the Asylum*. Boston: Little, Brown, 1971.

Rowland, Christopher. *The Cambridge Companion to Liberation Theology*. Cambridge: Cambridge University Press, 1999.

Ruether, Rosemary Radford, ed. *Gender, Ethnicity, and Religion: Views from the Other Side*. Minneapolis, MN: Fortress Press, 2002.

———. *Sexism and God-talk: Toward a Feminist Theology*. Boston: Beacon Press, 1983.

———. "A White Feminist Response to Black and Womanist Theologies." In *Living Stones in the Household of God*, ed. Linda E. Thomas, 51–58. Minneapolis, MN: Fortress Press, 2004.

Russell, Ronald. "Redemptive Suffering and Paul's Thorn in the Flesh." *Journal of the Evangelical Theological Society* 39 (1996): 565–566.

Saiving, Valerie C. "The Human Situation: A Feminine View." *Journal of Religion* 40 (1960): 100–112.

———. "Our Bodies/Our Selves: Reflections on Sickness, Aging, and Death." *Journal of Feminist Studies* 4 (1988): 117–125.

Sampley, J. Paul. "The Second Letter to the Corinthians." *New Interpreter's Bible*, vol. 11, 164–167. Nashville, TN: Abingdon Press, 1994.

Samuel, Vinay. "God, Humanity, and Disability." *Transformation* 15, no. 4 (1998): 15–17.

Sawyer, John F. A., ed. *Reading Leviticus: A Conversation with Mary Douglas.* Sheffield, UK: Sheffield Academic Press, 1996.

Saxton, Marsha, and Florence Howe, eds. *With Wings: An Anthology of Literature by and about Women with Disabilities.* New York: Feminist Press, 1987.

Scarry, Elaine. *The Body in Pain: The Making and Unmaking of the World.* Oxford: Oxford University Press, 1985.

Schipper, Jeremy. *Disability Studies and the Hebrew Bible: Figuring Mephibosheth in the David Story.* New York: T & T Clark, 2006.

Schiebinger, Londa, ed. *Feminism and the Body.* Oxford: Oxford University Press, 2000.

Schilling, Chris. *The Body and Social Theory.* London: Sage, 2003.

Schneider, Laurel C. *Re-imagining the Divine: Confronting the Backlash against Feminist Theology.* Cleveland, OH: Pilgrim Press, 1998.

Schrein, Shannon. *Quilting and Braiding: The Feminist Christologies of Sallie McFague and Elizabeth A. Johnson in Conversation.* Collegeville, MN: Liturgical Press, 1998.

Schüssler Fiorenza, Elisabeth. *Bread Not Stone: The Challenge of Feminist Biblical Interpretation.* Boston: Beacon Press, 1984.

———. *In Memory of Her: A Feminist Theological Reconstruction of Christian Origins.* New York: Crossroad, 1983.

———. "Paul and the Politics of Interpretation." In *Paul and Politics*, ed. Richard A. Horsley, 40–57. Harrisburg, PA: Trinity Press International, 2000.

Scully, Jackie Leach. "When Embodiment Isn't Good." *Theology and Sexuality* 9 (1998): 10–28.

Senior, Donald. "Beware of the Canaanite Woman: Disability and the Bible." In *Religion and Disability: Essays in Scripture, Theology, and Ethics*, ed. Marilyn Bishop, 1–26. Kansas City: Sheed and Ward, 1995.

Sheets-Johnstone, Maxine, ed. *Giving the Body Its Due.* Albany: State University of New York Press, 1992.

Shildrick, Margrit. *Leaky Bodies and Boundaries: Feminism, Postmodernism, and (Bio)Ethics.* London: Routledge, 1997.

Shildrick, Margrit, and Roxanne Mykitiuk, eds. *Ethics of the Body: Postconventional Challenges.* Cambridge, MA: MIT Press, 2005.

Shuman, Joel, and Brian Volk. *Reclaiming the Body: Christians and the Faithful Use of Modern Medicine.* Grand Rapids, MI: Brazos Books, 2006.

Smith, Bonnie, and Beth Hutchison, eds. *Gendering Disability.* New Brunswick, NJ: Rutgers University Press, 2004.

Snyder, Sharon L., Brenda Jo Brueggemann, and Rosemarie Garland Thomson, eds. *Disability Studies: Enabling the Humanities.* New York: Modern Language Association of America, 2002.

Sontag, Frederick. "Metaphorical Non-sequitur: Sallie McFague's Metaphorical Theology and Imagery for God." *Asia Journal of Theology* 11 (1997): 20–35.

Sontag, Susan. *Illness as Metaphor.* New York: Farrar, Straus and Giroux, 1978.

Stark, Rodney. "Epidemics, Networks, and the Rise of Christianity." *Semeia* 56 (1991): 159–175.

———. *The Rise of Christianity: A Sociologist Reconsiders History.* Princeton, NJ: Princeton University Press, 1996.

Stiker, Henri-Jacques. *Corps infirmes et sociétés.* Translated by William Sayers. Ann Arbor: University of Michigan Press, 1999.

Stuart, Elizabeth. "Disruptive Bodies: Disability, Embodiment and Sexuality." In *Good News of the Body: Sexual Theology and Feminism,* ed. Lisa Isherwood, 166–184. New York: New York University Press, 2000.

———. *Gay and Lesbian Theologies: Repetitions with Critical Difference.* Burlington, VT: Ashgate, 2003.

Stuart, Meryn, and Glynis Ellerington. "Unequal Access: Disabled Women's Exclusion from the Mainstream Women's Movement." *Women and Environments* 12, no. 2 (1990): 19.

Sugden, Chris. "Biblical and Theological Reflections on Disability." *Transformation* 15, no. 4 (1998): 27–30.

Swinton, John and Brian Brock, eds. *Theology, Disability, and the New Genetics: Why Science Needs the Church.* London: T & T Clark, 2007.

Tambornino, John. *The Corporeal Turn: Passion, Necessity, Politics.* Lanham, MD: Rowman and Littlefield, 2002.

———. "Disability and Christology in the Fourth Gospel." Ph.D. diss., Westminster Theological Seminary, 1994.

Tan, Amanda Shao. "The Disabled Christ." *Transformation* 15, no. 4 (1998): 8–14.

Tanner, Kathryn. Review of *Body of God,* by Sallie McFague. *Modern Theology* 10 (1994): 417–419.

Tatman, Lucy. *Knowledge That Matters: A Feminist Theological Paradigm and Epistemology.* Cleveland, OH: Pilgrim Press, 2001.

TeSelle, Sallie. *Literature and the Christian Life.* New Haven, CT: Yale University Press, 1966.

Thistlethwaite, Susan Brooks, ed. *Adam, Eve, and the Genome: The Human Genome Project and Theology.* Minneapolis, MN: Fortress Press, 2003.

Thistlethwaite, Susan Brooks, and Mary Potter Engel, eds. *Lift Every Voice: Constructing Christian Theologies from the Underside.* Maryknoll, NY: Orbis Books, 1998.

Thomas, Linda E., ed. *Living Stones in the Household of God.* Minneapolis, MN: Fortress Press, 2004.

Thomson, Rosemarie Garland. "Body Criticism as a Context for Disability Studies." *Disability Studies Quarterly* 17 (1997): 297–300.

———. *Extraordinary Bodies: Figuring Physical Disability in American Culture and Literature*. New York: Columbia University Press, 1997.

———. "Redrawing the Boundaries of Feminist Disability Studies." *Feminist Studies* 20 (1994): 583–596.

Tilley, Maureen A., and Susan A. Ross, eds. *Broken and Whole: Essays on Religion and the Body*. Lanham, MD: University Press of America, 1995.

Titchkosky, Tanya. *Disability, Self, and Society*. Toronto: University of Toronto Press, 2003.

Trent, James W., Jr. *Inventing the Feeble Mind: A History of Mental Retardation in the United States*. Berkeley: University of California Press, 1994.

Trible, Phyllis. *God and the Rhetoric of Sexuality*. Philadelphia: Fortress Press, 1978.

———. *Texts of Terror: Literary-Feminist Readings of Biblical Narratives*. Philadelphia: Fortress, 1984.

Turner, Bryan S. *The Body and Society: Explorations in Social Theory*. London: Sage, 1996.

———. "The Body in Western Society: Social Theory and Its Perspectives." In *Religion and the Body*, ed. Sarah Coakley, 15–41. Cambridge: Cambridge University Press, 1997.

Vanier, Jean. *The Challenge of L'Arche*. Ottawa: Novalis, 1981.

Ware, Kallistos. "My Helper and My Enemy: The Body in Greek Christianity." In *Religion and the Body*, ed. Sarah Coakley, 90–110. Cambridge: Cambridge University Press, 1997.

Webb, Stephen H. "Should We Love All of Nature? A Critique of Sallie McFague's *Super, Natural Christians*." *Encounter* 59 (1998): 409–419.

Webb-Mitchell, Brett. *Dancing with Disabilities: Opening the Church to All God's Children*. Cleveland, OH: United Church Press, 1996.

———. *God Plays Piano Too: The Spiritual Lives of Disabled Children*. New York: Crossroad, 1993.

———. "Making the Table Accessible." *Christian Ministry* 29 (1998): 14–16.

———. *Unexpected Guests at God's Banquet: Welcoming People with Disabilities into the Church*. New York: Crossroad, 1994.

Weissenrieder, Annette. *Images of Illness in the Gospel of Luke*. Tübingen: Mohr Siebeck, 2003.

Welch, Sharon D. "Sporting Power: American Feminism, French Feminism, and an Ethic of Conflict." In *Transfigurations: Theology and the French Feminists*, ed. C. W. Maggie Kim, Susan M. St. Ville, and Susan M. Simonaitis, 171–198. Minneapolis, MN: Augsburg Fortress, 1993.

———. *Sweet Dreams in America: Making Ethics and Spirituality Work*. New York: Routledge, 1999.

Wells, Harold. "The Flesh of God: Christological Implications for an Ecological Vision of the World." *Toronto Journal of Theology* 15 (1999): 51–68.

Wendell, Susan. *The Rejected Body: Feminist Philosophical Reflections on Disability*. New York: Routledge, 1996.

West, Cornel. "The New Cultural Politics of Difference." *October* 53 (1990): 93–109.

White, L. Michael, and O. Larry Yarbrough, eds. *The Social World of the First Christians: Essays in Honor of Wayne A. Meeks.* Minneapolis, MN: Fortress Press, 1995.

Wilbur, Ronnie. *American Sign Language: Linguistic and Applied Dimensions.* San Diego, CA: College Hill Press, 1987.

Wilke, Harold. *Creating the Caring Congregation.* Nashville, TN: Abingdon, 1980.

———. *Strengthened with Might.* Philadelphia: Westminster Press, 1952.

Willis, Kimberly Anne. "Claiming the 'Fearsome Possibility': Toward a Contextual Christology of Disability." In *Gender, Ethnicity, and Religion: Views from the Other Side,* ed. Rosemary Radford Ruether, 215–229. Minneapolis, MN: Fortress Press, 2002.

Wilson, James C., and Cynthia Lewiecki-Wilson, eds. *Embodied Rhetorics: Disability in Language and Culture.* Carbondale: Southern Illinois University Press, 2001.

Winter, S. C. "Why Is Christianity Anti-Body? Or Is It?" In *Putting Body and Soul Together: Essays in Honor of Robin Scroggs,* ed. Virginia Wiles, Alexandra Brown, and Graydon F. Snyder, 46–57. Valley Forge, PA: Trinity Press International, 1997.

Witt, Cynthia Beth Dehmlow. "Epistemology in the Theological Writings of Rosemary Radford Ruether, Sallie McFague and Carter Heyward." Ph.D. diss., Claremont Graduate University, 1995.

Wolfensberger, Wolf. *The Principle of Normalization in Human Services.* Toronto: National Institute on Mental Retardation, 1972.

Woodcock, Kathryn. "Cochlear Implants vs. Deaf Culture?" In *Deaf World: A Historical Reader and Primary Sourcebook,* ed. Lois Bragg, 325–332. New York: New York University Press, 2001.

Woods, Laurie. "Opposition to a Man and His Message: Paul's 'Thorn in the Flesh.'" *Australian Biblical Review* 39 (1991): 52.

Woodward, James. "Black Southern Signing." *Language in Society* 5 (1975): 211–218.

Yong, Amos. *Theology and Down Syndrome: Reimaging Disability in Late Modernity.* Waco, TX: Baylor University Press, 2007.

Zita, Jacquelyn N. *Body Talk: Philosophical Reflections on Sex and Gender.* New York: Columbia University Press, 1998.

Index

DATE DUE

DEMCO, INC. 38-2931